The A...

Then and Now

By Henry Jacobsen

This book is written with your reading enjoyment in mind, but a leader's guide, to facilitate use in study groups, is available at 95¢.

Published by

VICTOR BOOKS

a division of SP Publications, Inc.

Contents

To MARION

Wife   Helpmeet
Inspiration

Author's Note

Writing this book has been a great experience!

For several months I have spent almost all my free time reading and studying The Acts as never before. As I pondered over the text itself and intensively researched the content, The Acts came alive to me.

I felt almost as though I were living back in the exciting days of the Roman Empire—as if I were a companion of Paul and Barnabas as they set out together to take the Gospel to Asia Minor. I relived the excitement of the hazardous voyage Paul and Luke made to Rome, and their shipwreck on the Island of Malta. I had something of the feeling of triumph the early Christians must have felt as they faced the crude, harsh world of their day with their simple and profound belief that Jesus Christ had conquered death for them.

I hope this book will enable you to share my experience.

One of the greatest miracles of all time is the continued existence of the Christian Church.

That a handful of peasants, most of them lacking any formal education, could launch a movement that would upset the world (Acts 17:6) is, humanly speaking, impossible.

But it happened!

It is not exaggeration to assert that our educational system, our hospitals, our concern for the poor, our scientific progress, and any respect we have for government, justice, and human rights all derive, directly or indirectly, from the teachings and practice of Christianity. Civilization, as we know it, has followed the Cross.

The Early Church had no billion-dollar budget.

It hired no skilled public relations men. It had no mass media through which to promote its cause. Its organization was disarmingly simple.

How did it do so incredible a job?

A study of The Acts tells us. For here is the record of primitive Christianity. Here is the story of how the first Christians felt, what they believed, how they witnessed. And Dwight L. Moody once said, "The nearer we get to the apostolic spirit and methods, the more power we will have."

This doesn't mean that the methods the Church used in the first century will necessarily work well in the twentieth. We live in a world that is radically different from that of the first believers. We must evaluate The Acts in the light of the doctrinal portions of the New Testament, and isolate the principles that are valid for today.

And above all, we must depend on the power that motivated, directed, and enabled the Early Church—the power of the Holy Spirit of God.

I have tried to indicate, in each chapter, what seems to be most useful to individual Christians and to local churches of our own century. At the same time, I have tried to supply adequate historical detail to "carry" the narrative.

May you find, in The Acts, greater reality for your own personal experience and greater vitality for the work of your church!   Henry Jacobsen

Chronology of The Acts

Scholars do not agree as to the precise dates of all the events recorded in The Acts, and some date most of them a year or two earlier than indicated here. However, the chart will give you the approximate time periods between the various occurrences. The epistles were probably written as indicated.

A.D. 30 The Ascension (Acts 1:9-11)
       Pentecost (chap. 2)
   30-35 Events of Acts 2:44—6:7
       Lame man healed; first arrest (chaps. 3; 4)
       Ananias and Sapphira (chap. 5)
       Second arrest (5:18)
       First beating (5:40)
       Deacons chosen (6:1-17)
    35 Stephen slain (chaps. 6; 7)
       Ministry of Philip (chap. 8)
    36 Paul's conversion (chap. 9
       Visit to Arabia (Gal. 1)
       Return to Damascus (9:22)
    39 Visit to Jerusalem (9:26-29)
    40 Sent to Tarsus (9:30)
A.D. 41 Peter and Cornelius (chaps. 10; 11)
    42 Preaching to Antioch Gentiles (11:20-24)
    43 Paul goes from Tarsus to Antioch (11:25)
    44 James martyred; Peter in jail (chap. 12)
    45 First Missionary Journey (chaps. 13; 14)
  47-50 In Antioch "a long time" (14:26-28)
    50 Council at Jerusalem (chap. 15)
       Dispute, Paul and Barnabas (15:35-39)
       Second Missionary Journey begins

Asia Minor, Troas, Philippi (15:40—16:40)
51 Thessalonica, Berea, Athens (chap. 17)
Paul in Corinth (18:1-17) 1 THESSALONIANS
52   2 THESSALONIANS
53 Visit in Ephesus (18:18-21)
54 Second Missionary Journey ends (18:22)
54 Third Missionary Journey begins (18:23)
Galatia and Phrygia (18:23-28)
Apollos at Ephesus (18:24-28)
Paul in Ephesus (chap. 19)
56   1 & 2 CORINTHIANS
A.D. 57 Riot of silversmiths   GALATIANS; ROMANS
Paul in southern, northern Greece (20:1-3)
58 Passover at Philippi (20:4-6)
Week in Troas (20:7-12)
Farewell at Miletus (20:13-38)
Trip to Jerusalem (21:1-16)
Paul in Jerusalem (21:17-25)
Paul's arrest, defense (chaps. 21; 22)
Removal to Caesarea (chap. 23)
Hearing before Felix (chap. 24)
Paul in prison at Caesarea (24:2-7)
60 Hearing before Festus (25:1-12)
Hearing before Agrippa (25:13—26:32)
Departure for Italy (27:1-3)
Shipwreck on Malta (chaps. 27; 28)
61 Arrival at Rome (chap. 28)
First Roman imprisonment   PHILEMON
62   COLOSSIANS; EPHESIANS; PHILIPPIANS
63 Period of freedom begins
67   1 TIMOTHY, TITUS
68 Second Roman imprisonment   2 TIMOTHY
Execution

1
The Work
Goes On

Acts 1

Luke, who wrote the Third Gospel, also wrote The Acts. His first literary work is concerned with "all that Jesus began to do and teach" (Acts 1:1). His second production continues the record started in his Gospel. It outlines the continuation of the work of Jesus Christ as carried on in and through His people by the power of the Holy Spirit.

Have you ever thought what would have happened if Jesus had not been crucified, and if He had not risen from the dead? His work would have been limited to one single spot on the globe, during one single lifetime. While He was teaching, preaching, and healing in Palestine, He was not available anywhere else. When His brief lifetime was over, His ministry would have terminated for all time. The whole Christian Era would have had only the written record of what Jesus did and said while He was alive.

Because of our Lord's death and resurrection, no such limitations have restrained Him. Jesus has been working in the world, down through the centuries, not only in Palestine but wherever His people are. His Holy Spirit, in every believer, gives His people wisdom and power to do His work.

That's what Jesus had in mind when He said, "The works that I do shall [a believer] do also; and greater works than these shall he do, because I go to the Father" (John 14:12).

The Acts—sometimes referred to as "The Acts of the Holy Spirit"—is the record of how Jesus' ministry was continued by the early Christians. It tells how they launched out on the challenging assignment of evangelizing the hostile world. It tells how they lived out the life of the risen Christ. Here we see how Jesus worked simultaneously in thousands of places—wherever believers were doing God's will.

Perhaps you enjoy Franz Schubert's Symphony No. 8. It is called the "Unfinished Symphony" because it has only three parts instead of the traditional four movements.

The Acts is an unfinished book. It describes the ministry of the risen Christ (or the Holy Spirit) for only a few years of the first century. But the Holy Spirit is still at work in the world. The Christian Church, contrary to what some folks mistakenly think, is very much alive. The Lord's people are still carrying on the tremendous task that they started a few weeks after the Resurrection.

Without the Resurrection, of course, there would have been no Acts. The apostles preached, taught, and worked miracles only in the power of the risen Christ. The Resurrection was their dynamic.

To early Christians the Resurrection was no mere doctrinal proposition. They didn't "think" or "hope" it was true. Jesus had showed Himself alive to them (Acts 1:3), convincing them beyond any trace of doubt that He was *living*. They knew why His grave was empty! They were eyewitnesses of the best-attested fact in ancient history. It is what makes Christianity unique among the "religions" of the world; none other can boast a risen Saviour!

Told to Wait

Jesus' command to His disciples, after His resurrection, was "Wait!"

Once they had seen their risen Lord, His followers undoubtedly wanted to get back to Galilee as fast as possible. That's where their friends were. Jerusalem was the last place in the world for them; the city was full of their enemies. The scribes were there, and the Pharisees, the Sadducees, and the multitudes whom the religious leaders had incited to demand Jesus' death (Matt. 27:20). It was not easy to wait in Jerusalem!

But then, it's *never* easy to wait—at least not until the inertia of old age overtakes us. Most of us normally want to be *doing* something.

This trait, sometimes called *drive*, or *ambition*, or *initiative*, is usually commendable.

But Jesus said Wait! "Wait for what the Father had promised. . . . You shall be baptized with the Holy Spirit not many days from now" (Acts 1:4, 5).

Not only the Father, but Jesus Himself, had promised that the Holy Spirit would come to teach, direct, and empower His people (John 14:16, 17). It was therefore imperative that they stay on at Jerusalem until they received the Spirit, without whom they would have been poorly equipped to do God's work (cf. Zech. 4:6).

Christians today need not "tarry" for the Spirit to enter their lives. When a person becomes a

Christian, he is baptized into the Church, the body of Christ, by the Holy Spirit (1 Cor. 12:13). Every believer *has* the Spirit. If a person doesn't have the Spirit, he isn't a Christian at all (Rom. 8:9).

But there are *other* reasons why some Christians need to "wait."

• Some need *training*. The apostles had been with Jesus for three years of the best training ever given prospective Christian workers.

It is tragic to put a Sunday School lesson quarterly in the hands of a new Christian who is willing to teach but knows nothing about teaching, and turn him loose on a class of children. The average Sunday School teacher is almost completely untrained. The remedy is not for such teachers to give up their classes, but for them to attend teacher training sessions or read up on the nature and methods of teaching.

• Some Christians need a measure of *maturity*. Paul cautions against the ordination of an immature Christian (1 Tim. 5:22) who has had no time to grow in grace or knowledge. A new convert today, especially if he comes out of a lurid and particularly unsavory past, is sometimes given more prominence than a seasoned believer.

• Some Christians need to wait because it is simply not yet *God's time* for the activity in which they will be involved. Joseph sat for months in an Egyptian prison cell. Moses spent 40 years in the backside of the desert. Our Lord Jesus Himself waited until he was about 30 years old before it was God's time for Him to begin His ministry.

Much of our Christian service is marred by our lack of awareness of God's timing. It is sinful for a Christian to drag his feet when God says "Go!" But it is equally sinful for him to rush on ahead of God. To act prematurely and in the flesh is to invite failure.

Unanswered Curiosity

The apostles were curious about prophecy, and in their last conversation with Jesus before His ascension they asked Him when He was going to set up the Kingdom (Acts 1:6). He did not rebuke them, but neither did He answer their question. He simply told them that this matter was something about which they need not be concerned.

Never before have Christians seemed as certain as they seem today that the Lord's coming is near —and of course it *is* 1,900 years nearer now than it was at Pentecost. It isn't wrong to be keenly interested in this subject, for Christ's return is our "blessed hope" and is to motivate us to personal purity (1 John 3:3) and to diligent and faithful service (Matt. 24:44).

To be obsessively preoccupied with Christ's return, however, is wrong. Some Christians read only books and magazine articles that deal with eschatology. They drive miles to hear a prominent prophetic teacher. They want to know not only *what* but *where* and *when*.

We *ought* to be knowledgeable about the Second Coming, but our major responsibilities are to allow this belief to change our lives and to tell other people about the One whose coming we expect. Christians are to be His "witnesses" (Acts 1:8).

A witness doesn't deal in hearsay. He doesn't tell what he thinks or suspects. He tells only what he *knows*. He limits himself to what he has personally seen and heard.

How do *you* rate as a witness? What can you

tell about what God has done for and in you? Is your firsthand Christian experience limited to something that happened years ago when you were saved, or has God been a living reality to you ever since?

One elderly man, asked for his testimony, told how when he was 18 months old God saved his life when he swallowed a safety pin. This was his most memorable experience with God.

What has God done for you this year? This month? This week? *Today?*

God is a *present* help. He is available to us here and now. He wants others to hear, from us, about our continuing contacts with Him.

Plan of Action

Before Jesus left His followers, He gave them a plan of action for doing God's work. This plan is a sort of geographical outline of The Acts. Christians were to witness first in Jerusalem (chaps. 1—7), then in Judea and Samaria (chaps. 8—12), and then in the uttermost parts of the earth: Asia Minor (chaps. 13—15), Greece (chaps. 16—23), and Rome (chaps. 24—28).

That's only the beginning, too. The Acts doesn't tell anything about taking the Gospel to northern Europe, to the other continents, and to the islands of the sea. But then, as we have said, The Acts is an unfinished book. You and I, hopefully, are still involved in carrying out the Lord's commission. And The Acts has given us the pattern, the master plan. It shows us the "how" of doing the job.

Your job isn't to start at Jerusalem—it's to begin *where you are. That's* "Jerusalem" for you. Christianity, like charity, is to start at home.

A recently converted college girl attended an Inter-Varsity Christian Fellowship conference in another city. She roomed with a family of Christians. "It was my first experience in a Christian home," she wrote to a friend. "The house was simple and so were the people, but you couldn't escape feeling that God was real to them on an everyday basis."

Would a visitor get that impression of *your* home?

After a Christian has practiced his faith in loving the members of his family (his Jerusalem), he is ready to represent Christ in the neighborhood (his "Judea"). And then he can witness at the office ("Samaria") and, finally, wherever he goes. But he should start at home.

After Jesus had ascended before the eyes of the apostles, they saw two angelic beings, dressed in white, standing nearby. These angels promised that Jesus would in due season return from heaven in the same manner as He had departed. That is, He would return corporeally and visibly (Acts 1: 11). His return is to be no mere subjective, "spiritual" affair.

Jesus' followers strained their eyes to follow Him as He went up. Then He was gone. They were alone. Even the angels had left. But the disciples understood clearly what the Lord wanted them to do. They were to tell about the risen Christ to the uttermost parts of the earth.

Those men did not know North and South America even existed, and they knew little about Asia, Africa, and even Europe. At that, the enormity of their assignment must have staggered them. It may be that some of them thought, "The job is impossible!" All of them must have wondered how they could possibly do it.

Sober and silent, they returned to Jerusalem, to the upstairs room where they were staying (Acts 1:12, 13). They were about 120 in number, including 11 apostles and a number of women.

Letting God Choose

Peter, always quick to act when action was necessary (and sometimes when it wasn't), proposed that the group must replace Judas to fill the ranks of the Twelve. Judas, overcome with hopeless remorse after he had betrayed Jesus, had committed suicide.

The man chosen, said Peter, should be a man who had been with the apostles from the beginning and who had seen the risen Christ (Acts 1:21, 22).

Two men with these qualifications were "nominated," and after prayer had been offered, lots were cast so that God (Prov. 16:33) might choose between the two candidates. The lot fell on Matthias.

For a church to select its officers by lot, on the basis of Acts 1, would hardly be acceptable in most quarters today. Usually church officers are elected by majority vote. Some churches have self-perpetuating governing boards. Other assemblies of believers claim that the Holy Spirit Himself selects the men who are to be their officers. They feel that the Spirit burdens the hearts of these men and that He makes them acceptable to those already in office. This may sound rather vague and impractical and hard to understand, but it seems to work rather well.

Some people believe that Paul, rather than

Matthias, was Judas' *real* successor. They point out that we never hear of Matthias again. But then, we never hear again of several others of the original Twelve. And additional apostles—including Barnabas (Acts 14:14) and James (1 Cor. 15:7)—were later chosen. The important principle here is that the Eleven did not elect a new apostle—they let God choose him.

Keep in mind, as you study The Acts, that this is a book of history, not of doctrine. Some of the actions recorded here are based on principles still applicable today, but others are not necessarily as valid in *our* world as they were in the simple culture of the first century. One must be discriminating and discerning in using The Acts as a guide for the Church today.

For example, the early Christians had to "wait" for the Holy Spirit, but since Pentecost such waiting is unnecessary. And the apostles cast lots to allow God to determine the choice of Matthias, but today there are more acceptable ways of selecting church officers, and there *are no apostles*.

When you study The Acts with this "restriction" in mind, it is a fascinating book. It reveals the secret of the great "success"—in matters important to God—of a generation of believers who lived and died to the glory of the Lord.

2
Witness
That Works
Acts 2

When you set out on a motor trip, you probably like your car's gas tank to be full. You like to begin your trip abroad with a good supply of traveler's checks.

The risen Christ gave His followers a tremendous "itinerary." They were to tell about Him to the uttermost parts of the earth. But He also promised to provision them and to give them all the power they would need (Acts 1:8).

Fifty days after the Resurrection, the Lord's promise was fulfilled. During the ten days since His ascension, 120 of the disciples had waited (Acts 1:4) in Jerusalem, talking about Him and His teachings and praying together. A feeling of unity and expectancy came over them. They were freed from the petty jealousies and personal rivalries that had at times disrupted their fellowships. When Christians meet together in this spirit, we may expect something wonderful to happen.

What took place must have been exciting! There was a sudden blast of violent, rushing wind. Then an overpowering wave of crimson flame surged into the room and settled on the heads of the believers.

Filled with the Spirit!

Some of these Christians had heard John the Baptist say that Jesus would baptize with the Holy Spirit and with fire (Luke 3:16). Pentecost fulfilled this prediction, for along with the fire that rested on these early saints came the compelling fullness of the Spirit of God, the only adequate source of the wisdom and power men need to do the Lord's work effectively.

Some may think the fullness of the Holy Spirit is only for pastors, missionaries, and perhaps Sunday School teachers. Not so! "They were *all* filled with the Holy Spirit" (Acts 2:4).

God's command, "Keep being filled with the Spirit" (Eph. 5:18, lit.), is for *every* Christian. It is for *you!*

The disciples had *received* the Holy Spirit before Jesus' ascension (John 20:22), but now they were *filled* with Him. Being filled with the Spirit doesn't mean you have more of Him—it means He has more of you. He has *all* of you. Your selfish will, your carnal ambitions, your personal pride are set aside, and you surrender to God.

As the disciples went out into the street, a strange phenomenon took place. They were talking earnestly, but not in any languages they had ever learned!

Bystanders who heard them recognized them, probably by their clothes, as Galileans (Acts 2:7), but each out-of-towner heard them in his own native foreign tongue, proclaiming God's mighty deeds (v. 11).

The disciples' ability to speak in unlearned

languages, on this occasion, was closely associated with the fullness of the Holy Spirit (v. 4).

Notice that there is nothing in this passage about speaking in "an unknown tongue"—about making utterances that mean nothing in any known language. There is nothing here about speaking in "the tongues of . . . angels." The "tongues" spoken by these first Christians were real human *languages,* and were understood by those who heard them.

Some of the hearers thought the Christians were drunk. (It is hard to understand why they should have associated intoxication with linguistic facility!)

Such was Pentecost, the birth of the Christian Church. It marked the time when the Holy Spirit came to abide in the hearts of God's people (John 14:16). The event has never been repeated, any more than the Incarnation or the Resurrection were repeated. The coming of the Holy Spirit to the Christian Church was a once-for-all event.

Preaching with Power

Peter had denied his Lord, but now, wholly committed to Jesus Christ and filled with the Spirit, he was a different man. Always ready to do *something,* Peter stepped up and preached to the bewildered crowd. He had no sermon notes, but he had two things that were infinitely more important. He had something to say, and he had the power of the Spirit.

Peter's message was typical of the sermons recorded in The Acts. Someone has suggested a five-point outline for it:

• *What Jesus did:* He worked miracles, wonders, and signs.

• *What you did:* You killed Him.

• *What God did:* He raised Jesus from the dead.

• *What we are doing now:* We are telling you the Good News that there is life for you in Christ.

• *What you can do:* You can turn to God through faith in His Son.

It was foolish, said Peter, as he began to speak, to think that his companions were drunk. No one would be drunk at 9 o'clock in the morning. What was going on fulfilled the prophecy of Joel about the pouring out of God's Spirit on mankind (vv. 17-21; Joel 2:28-32). Joel had also mentioned wonders, signs, and celestial disturbances that will not take place until the "Day of the Lord"—the time of judgment—approaches. Pentecost was only a partial fulfillment of his prophecy.

Peter's quotation from Joel closed with the encouraging news that everyone who calls on the name of the Lord will be saved (Acts 2:21).

Though Peter wanted his hearers to ask God for salvation, he didn't "butter them up" with flattering words. He said that Jesus' miracles had amply proved His deity and that the Jews had been well aware of this. However, they had had Jesus nailed to the cross by the hands of the godless Romans (cf. vv. 22, 23). It is as foolish to deny that the Jews of Peter's day were responsible for killing Jesus as it is to blame His death on the Jews of our own generation.

But the Jews and the Romans were able to crucify the Son of God only because His death was part of God's predetermined plan (v. 23). The Lamb of God *had* to die for the sins of all the world.

The grave could not hold our Lord, continued Peter, quoting David's prediction of the Resurrection (v.v. 25-28; Ps. 16:8-11). The disciples had themselves *seen* the risen Christ.

When a preacher speaks in the power of the Holy Spirit, his hearers are likely to be "convicted." They face themselves as God sees them and realize their sinfulness.

Peter's hearers were pierced to the heart.

"Brothers!" they inquired, "what shall we do?"

Peter didn't tell them to "get religion" or to mend their ways. He told them to repent.

To repent means to change one's mind about God and His holiness, about sin, and about oneself. It means more than to be sorry for sin. It means taking God's view of it.

Peter also told his hearers to be baptized in the name of Jesus Christ. Baptism is a way of confessing one's faith in the Lord Jesus. Peter's hearers were baptized because they had put their trust in the Saviour.

Salvation is for all classes (v. 39), old and young, parent and child. Don't be frightened by the qualifying phrase, "as many as the Lord our God shall call to Himself." It doesn't contradict the promise, "Every one who calls on the name of the Lord shall be saved" (v. 21).

As the result of the Spirit's convicting power, Peter's sermon led about 3,000 persons to call on God for salvation.

The Church's Job

But conversion is not an end, it is merely a beginning. "Being saved" is only the first step on a long road—the Christian life.

The Christians saved on the Day of Pentecost seem to have realized this. They were "continually devoting themselves to the apostles' teaching and to fellowship, to the breaking of bread, and to prayer" (v. 42).

These men and women had done far more than assent intellectually to the truth Peter had proclaimed. Their being baptized identified them permanently with the original "Jesus Movement." It involved them in total commitment to a whole new way of life.

Notice the elements prominent in the work of the Early Church—elements indispensable in any age if the Church is to do its work well:

• *Teaching.* Being a Christian is much more than believing a set of doctrinal propositions. A Christian is a person in whom Christ lives. But this experience is based on the truth God has revealed in the Bible. The better a person knows this truth, the more intelligent and effective a believer he can be. That's why it is so important that the Church *teach* its members, both in Sunday School and from the pulpit. Proper instruction is absolutely essential.

• *Fellowship.* Christians urgently need the company of others who know and love the Lord, especially when they are new converts. A believer is part of the body of Christ. Other members of the body are to help him, and he them (Rom. 12:4-8). He needs to be with Christians, to talk with them, and to worship and learn and work with them. Christian fellowship, in which God's people share their joys and sorrows, their successes and failures, and their insights in the Word, is tremendously important to a believer's healthy spiritual growth.

• *The breaking of bread.* This is probably a reference to the Lord's Supper (cf. v. 46). The

Early Church may have observed this act of worship daily.

• *Prayer.* We sing about "the pure delight of a single hour that before Thy throne we spend," but most of us really prefer an extra hour of sleep. Because God was so real to the early Christians, their praying was natural and enjoyable. We shall see, in later studies, how they prayed and what they asked for.

There's no mention here of *evangelism.* When the early Christians came together to learn, worship, pray, and fellowship, it's not likely that they listened to evangelistic messages on the plan of salvation. The New Testament gives no support to the idea that the local church is a soul-saving station where the pastor discharges his people's responsibility to witness to the lost. A steady diet of evangelistic preaching can grow spindly saints who know little or nothing about the "strong meat" of the Word.

The Early Church *was* evangelistic, to be sure. Those hardy Christians preached the Gospel in the synagogues where unbelieving Jews would hear it, on the street corners in the hearing of all, and in homes that were open to them. But they would not have tried to evangelize a Sunday evening congregation composed entirely of saints.

It's impossible, in reading The Acts, to escape the conclusion that early Christians looked on the meetings of the local church as being conducted for the benefit of God's people. There they were taught and trained, there they shared and worshiped, and there they prayed together. Then they went out into marketplace and byways, telling others about the wonders of this new Way of life.

"Everyone kept feeling a sense of awe" (v. 43).

They sensed keenly the reality of God. Such spiritual vitality today may not produce the kind of wonders and signs that the apostles worked, but where Christians are filled with God's Spirit, sinners are saved, lives are changed, prayer is effective, and missions flourish. These are modern "wonders and signs."

The early believers proved their sincerity by the way they treated poverty-stricken fellow Christians. "They began selling their property and possessions, and were sharing them with all, as anyone might have need" (v. 45). When a person's faith goes beyond lip service and affects his pocketbook, we *know* it's for real!

This so-called "communism" of the Early Church had nothing in common with today's Communism. It had a spiritual basis, not a materialistic one. Its followers were believers, not atheists. Its purpose was to glorify God, not to deny Him. Its giving was voluntary, not compulsory.

The first Christians clung to the Temple, which had been the focus of their religious life as Jews. Their homes, however, also became central in their religious activities. Church buildings were unknown, and believers gathered from house to house for prayer, the Lord's Supper, fellowship, and teaching (v. 46).

Home Bible classes, growing in popularity today, are a return to this sort of activity, and promise to be an important factor in present-day church renewal and revival.

Do you know Christians who are unpopular with their neighbors? Such individuals aren't like the first-century Christians, who enjoyed "favor with all the people" (v. 47). They were a happy, friendly, helpful lot of people, and others instinctively took to them. Only later did unpopularity and persecution arise. It was instigated and cultivated by the individuals who incited the Jerusalem Passover crowd to demand Jesus' crucifixion—by the leaders of the religious establishment.

The Early Church grew rapidly, and new members were added day by day.

These new believers were added as they "were being saved" (v. 47). There is no suggestion that church membership was withheld from new converts until they had given up practices that some believers regarded as carnal or worldly. The Early Church apparently believed that with continued instruction and Christian fellowship, any really unspiritual beliefs or habits wouldn't survive long.

The scriptural requirement for membership in the body of Christ is salvation—not spiritual maturity.

3
Preaching That Persuades

Acts 3

Henry Ward Beecher was one of this country's most gifted and effective preachers. After he was graduated from seminary, however, and had taken a church in what was then called the "Indiana Wilderness," he was dismayed to find that few people came to hear him preach and still fewer paid any attention to what he said.

Beecher turned to his Bible for encouragement, determined to find in it what he was doing wrong.

He read in The Acts about the tremendous effectiveness of the Early Church. He asked himself, "What was the secret of it? What did *they* do that *I* am not doing? What can I learn here for *my* ministry?"

He searched out the principles behind apostolic witnessing and preaching, by which thousands of men and women were brought into the Kingdom.

Beecher's ministry was revolutionized. The first Sunday he applied the principles he had discovered, 17 men responded to his invitation.

Acts 3 contains the second of Peter's recorded sermons. Even if you are not a preacher, this passage will speak to you. It contains the principles by which God brings people under conviction as you witness to them.

This sermon was preceded by a miracle.

John and Peter, always good friends, were going to the Temple at 3 o'clock in the afternoon, the hour of prayer. The Jews—even those who had become Christians—prayed regularly four times a day, setting an example for us modern believers. (We think we have more "practical" things to occupy us!)

A crippled man, lame from birth, was being set down at the Temple gate by his friends. He made his living begging. The Temple gate was a good location, and no doubt he realized how lucky he was to have friends to carry him there and back each day.

As the cripple began to ask for alms, Peter interrupted him. "Look at us!" (v. 4) the apostle commanded.

The beggar looked up, no doubt anticipating a generous handout.

"I have no money," said Peter—and we can almost feel the man's quick loss of interest—"but I give you what I have. In the name of Jesus Christ the Nazarene—walk!" (cf. v. 6)

Then, seizing the man's wrists, Peter pulled him upright.

It's fine to tell a cripple to get up, but it's even better to help him to his feet. It's fine to give a person good advice, but the touch of a helping hand will warm the heart more than any amount of counsel. How about it? Do we get *involved* with the people we want to reach?

The cripple's ankles were miraculously strengthened at once. He walked and jumped in sheer

ecstasy, and entered the Temple with his benefactors, praising God.

Everyone who saw it was amazed.

Timely Topic

A preacher is at an advantage when his sermon
is preceded by a miracle, but let's not be too down-
hearted. One of the most effective miracles is a
life transformed by the power of God. Christian
courage and cheerfulness and love, if they are elements of our personality, will pave the way for
our testimony, too.

Peter was an opportunist in the good sense of
the word. He capitalized on the attention the
miracle had created and used it as the text of a
Gospel sermon.

A sermon—or a testimony—is often better received if it is linked to something everyone is
talking about. The president's visit to China, the
vandalism of the Pieta at the Vatican, or a nearby
forest fire—these are all good "attention getters."

A message is also more effective if it convinces
people that God can meet *their* present needs:
loneliness, disappointment, worry, frustration, re-
sentment, fear, hate, or whatever.

This principle is known as "talking to people
where they are." Peter, in Acts 2 and 3, showed
himself a master at doing this.

The apostle began by commenting on the
miracle, a subject of keen interest right then to
his hearers. He disclaimed any credit for healing
the lame man and pointed out clearly that the
healing was done in the power of the name of
Jesus Christ (v. 16).

Peter's sermon began with Christ, and that's

where it also ended (v. 26). In fact, it was about Christ from beginning to end.

Peter didn't mention poverty, or sickness, or slavery, or high taxes, or government tyranny, or racism, or the oppression of the poor by the rich, though all these problems bothered the world at that time. Peter preached Christ.

The New Testament has lots to say on *moral* issues in the economic, social, and political realms, but it says it *to Christians*. Peter was not preaching to Christians—he was talking *to unbelievers*. He knew that what the men and women listening to him needed more than anything else was to receive Christ. Time enough, *after* people have been converted, after they become members of God's family, to instruct them in their other obligations.

• Peter glorified Christ, showing that He is vitally related to the God of Abraham, Isaac, and Jacob (v. 13), whom the Jews revered. He called Jesus "the Holy and Righteous One" (v. 14) and "the Prince of life" (v. 15). He explained that it was through faith in Christ that the crippled man had been given "perfect health" (v. 16).

Placing the Blame

• Peter faced his hearers frankly with their sin. They, or other Jews whose views they shared, had insisted, just a few weeks before, that Pontius Pilate release Barabbas, a murderer, when the Roman procurator wanted to turn Jesus loose (vv. 13, 14; Matt. 27:21, 22). Through their unbelief and rejection, they were responsible for their Messiah's crucifixion (Acts 3:15).

The apostle conceded that the people and their rulers had acted in ignorance (v. 17), but their ignorance was inexcusable. The Jews, and especially their religious leaders, had the testimony of the Old Testament and should have recognized their Messiah when He appeared.

• Peter mentioned some of this Old Testament evidence (v. 22). Moses, who delivered Israel from Egypt, had foretold the coming of a Prophet like himself. All the Hebrew prophets (v. 24) had proclaimed the same truth. Daniel had given even the time of Messiah's coming (Dan. 9:24-27), and his prophecy was common knowledge among the scribes. But they found the control of their nation's religion a lucrative prize. They chose to ignore prophecy because they didn't want their pleasant routine interrupted by a Messiah who might upset their applecart.

They were like the people, today, who aren't interested in Christ's return because they want to go on indefinitely in their pleasant way of life. A nice split-level home, a cushy job with a thumping good salary and a great pension, lots of interesting friends—who's hankering for the Lord's return, anyway?

• Peter also preached the Resurrection (vv. 15, 26). The energizing truth that Christ is alive was the very foundation of apostolic preaching and witnessing. This is the truth that makes Christianity unique. It gives believers "something to talk about."

• Peter again urged his hearers to repent (v. 19; cf. 2:38). He pleaded with them to return to God. Personal faith in Jesus Christ is clearly in view in Moses' prediction: To Him the people of Israel were to give heed in everything He said (v. 22). This prediction implies obedience to Jesus' message. And part of Jesus' message is that men do God's will by believing in the Christ whom God sent (cf. John 6:29).

And there is no acceptable alternative to "heeding" Jesus by putting one's confidence in Him as the Saviour He asserted Himself to be. Those who fail to do so face utter destruction (Acts 3:23).

• Peter wanted his hearers to accept his message "in order that times of refreshing may come from the presence of the Lord; and that He may send Jesus . . . whom heaven must receive until the period of restoration of all things" (vv. 19-21). Some take these words to mean that when the appointed number of souls has come to Christ in personal faith, He will return and set up His kingdom. That will be a time of unparalleled peace and blessing—a time when God's promise to Abraham (v. 25) will be entirely fulfilled.

Unfinished But Successful

Peter never finished his sermon. He was interrupted by an irate delegation of Sadducees and Temple guards. In spite of this rudeness on the part of the establishment, however, many people embraced Christianity as a result of hearing the apostle's message (cf. 4:4). We must admit that Peter's sermon was a success!

Why did Peter's sermon get such results?

Peter had preached in the power of the omnipotent Holy Spirit, the only Force in the universe who can convict men and draw them to Christ. His message was soundly scriptural (vv. 18, 22-25). His points were drawn from and supported by the Word of God rather than from some popular philosopher or psychiatrist. He told his hearers about the person and work of Jesus Christ and proved our Lord's deity by the Resurrection. He faced His hearers with their sin, especially the sin of rejecting Christ. He urged them to repent and turn to God through faith in Christ, and he warned them that the options before them were belief and blessing on the one hand and rejection and destruction on the other.

These are still the elements of effective preaching and witnessing.

But don't worry if your presentation of the Gospel doesn't convince 2,000 persons, or two, or even one. Numerical success is up to the Holy Spirit, who does the "regenerating," or giving of the new birth. If you tell the message faithfully, lovingly, and tactfully, your witness is successful. Leave "results" to God!

It was about 3 o'clock (3:1) when Peter began to preach. It was "already evening" (4:3) when he was interrupted. He had talked for at least two or three hours.

But then, Peter wasn't preaching to people exposed to radio, television, and the printed page. Folks of his day were hungry for all they could hear, and gladly listened to a public speaker for almost any length of time. Anyone who tries to preach for two or three hours today will soon learn that sermon-length is one area where he had better not imitate Peter.

And here's a final key to Peter's "results": Peter was talking to an audience made up largely of unsaved individuals. We saw (chap. 2) that the Early Church made a point of preaching evangelistic sermons *where there were unsaved persons to hear them*. The first rule for successful fishing is to let down your line where the fish are!

We must face the fact that unsaved people do

not flock to church today. If they come at all, they usually don't come to the evening service. Unsaved people today are to be found in their homes watching TV, at shopping centers, golf courses, lakes, campgrounds. Those are the places where we must give the message about Jesus and His salvation.

That's how they did it in the days of The Acts. When we get to chapter 20, we'll examine the kind of sermon the apostles preached to a group of *believers*. It was definitely *not* evangelistic.

The great evangelistic sermons recorded in the early chapters of The Acts were not preached to gatherings that were predominantly Christian. They were not delivered at church services. They were preached on the streets or at the Temple, and those who heard them were, for the most part, unsaved men and women.

We can learn a lot from the apostles at this point.

4
Facing Opposition

Acts 4

When someone asked D. L. Moody if he had enough grace to be burned at the stake, he said, "No."

"Don't you wish you had?" he was asked.

"No," he said, "because I don't need it. What I need right now is enough grace to live in Milwaukee for the next three days."

We may never have to face the hardships endured by the apostles, all but one of whom, tradition says, died as martyrs. But we will need grace for the testings that will come our way. Christians are not exempt from such trials as sickness, accidents, bereavements, disappointments, and the like, but their resources in Christ can abundantly enable them to bear with grace whatever comes their way.

Trouble wasn't long in coming to the Early Church. Peter's second sermon precipitated the first wave of anti-Christian persecution. Before he finished his message late in the afternoon, a contingent of the Temple guards, accompanied by priests and Sadducees, descended on him and put him under arrest.

The Sadducees were the "liberal" theologians of that day. They rejected the supernatural and declared that resurrection was a scientific impossibility. They strongly favored keeping on good terms with the Roman overlords of Palestine, and for this reason they could tolerate no movement that involved a national leader such as the Messiah was expected to be. Such "sedition" would bring down the wrath of Rome and must therefore be squelched at all costs.

When Peter and John were arrested, it was too late in the afternoon to do anything. So Peter and John cooled their heels in jail overnight. But this interruption didn't hinder the effectiveness of Peter's preaching, and enough persons were saved to bring the total adult male membership of the Church to 5,000 (v. 4).

Persecution of Christians, far from hindering church growth, has often fostered it. Perhaps when Christians take trouble in their stride, unbelievers become convinced that God and Christianity are realities worth considering.

The next day the two apostles faced an imposing court of inquiry, convened in accordance with Moses' law (Deut. 13:1-5). They were asked (Acts 4:7) what power had enabled them to heal the cripple the previous afternoon.

Accusing the Accusers

Peter made no effort at all to defend himself or John. Speaking for both of them, he stated plainly that the healing had been performed by the power of the name of Christ.

And then he went on to accuse their accusers. There may be a time for a nice, inoffensive testimony that will ruffle no feathers and give no offense. There is a time to be subtle and discreet. But there are also times for a hard-hitting, forthright presentation of the whole truth, even when it is certain to infuriate someone.

Only the Holy Spirit can direct you as to which approach is right on a given occasion.

The Holy Spirit led Peter to be blunt.

You crucified Jesus, he charged. He is the Stone which you have rejected but which has become the very Cornerstone of the building (cf. vv. 10, 11).

Peter's hearers would understand that he was alluding to the old legend about the building of the Temple. The huge stones for it were shaped at the quarry so that as the edifice was constructed there would be no noise caused by the hammers of stonemasons. When one particular stone arrived on the scene, the builders laid it aside. They thought it had been cut to the wrong size and shape. Later, to everyone's surprise, this stone turned out to be the keystone of one of the walls.

Jesus is foundational in God's plan, Peter was saying, and your rejection of Him does not alter this fact!

Christ is not optional. He is not one of several saviours from among whom men may choose. "There is salvation in no one else" (v. 12).

After Harry Ironside, the great preacher of a generation ago, had been converted, he waded through 38 ponderous volumes about the various religions of mankind. He was struck by the truth that only Christianity holds out the promise of a Saviour who gave Himself for lost men and women.

There are actually ministers in Christian pulpits today who preach that a person may find salvation in Islam, Buddhism, Christian Science, or almost anything else, if only he is sincere. Such diabolical heresies have led many astray and are directly opposed to the teachings of the New Testament. They are promoted by men who are willfully blind to the great underlying truth that this is God's universe and that He writes the rules. Man is simply not free to pick and choose for himself which "religion" is "right for me," and to ignore the only One who can save.

Impressive Confidence

The ecclesiastical court marveled (v. 13) at the boldness and confidence of Peter and John. The two apostles were untrained men, without much formal education, and their judges recognized that both of them had been in the band that followed Jesus around the country during His ministry.

The court was embarrassed, too, by the presence of the healed man (v. 14), who had come to attend the trial of his benefactors. With the evidence standing right there in front of them, it was impossible for them to deny that a remarkable miracle had been performed (v. 16).

The dignitaries did what boards and committees have always done when facing an impasse. They went into executive session (v. 15) and tried to resolve their problem.

Then they called Peter and John back and let them off with a suspended sentence. They were to do no more preaching or teaching in the name of Jesus (v. 18).

The purpose of the sentence was to stifle the truth. The officials did not *deny* the miracle, but they refused to *accept* its implications. They had made up their minds, and they were not going to be confused with mere facts. As far as they were concerned, Jesus was dead, buried, and of no further interest. They closed their eyes to any new evidence.

People today do the same thing when, faced with the Gospel and the evidence of changed lives, they simply refuse to believe. They apparently fail to realize that a fact remains a fact whether they believe it or not. Closing your eyes to an obstacle will not help you to avoid stumbling over it. And facts don't "go away" by your shutting your eyes to them.

Peter was not a man to be easily discouraged.

You decide, he told the court, whether it is right for us to obey you rather than God. We simply can't *help* telling about what we have seen and heard (cf. vv. 19, 20).

The relationship between a Christian and the authorities is outlined quite clearly in Romans 13. In God's sight, the purpose of government is to preserve order by restraining evil and promoting good. This does not mean that God approves of all the actions of any given government. It means that every true government is set up under the controlling providence of God. No Christian has a right to refuse to obey the authorities because he doesn't approve of their regulations. The man did wrong who, sure that the authorities had made a mistake in making his block a one-way street, *insisted* on approaching his home from the wrong direction.

When there is a *bona fide* conflict, however, between God's will and governmental decree, a Christian's duty is to obey God, as in the case of Peter and John. Christ had commanded that His disciples witness, starting at Jerusalem, and the authorities flatly told them they were not to do so. The disciples saw their duty clearly enough.

After they had been released, Peter and John joined their fellow Christians and gave them a full report of what had happened.

Then the whole group had a prayer meeting. For what would *you* have prayed?

Would you have asked for vengeance on the religious leaders who had persecuted you? Would you have asked protection for yourself and your fellow Church members? That would have been pretty reasonable, wouldn't it?

Asking for Boldness

The first thing these Christians did was to worship God (vv. 24-28). They glorified Him as Creator of the universe, and recalled David's prophecy, fulfilled before their eyes, of the opposition that would come (vv. 25, 26; Ps. 2:1, 2).

When we *worship* God, we *concentrate* on Him. We lose ourselves in adoration and praise of the One who is infinite, sovereign, all-loving, omnipotent, and good. As we focus our attention on Him, our problems become, relatively, smaller and smaller.

The early Christians admitted to God (vv. 27, 28) that His enemies had done only what He had allowed them to do. Even when things go wrong, our sovereign God is on the throne of the universe and is in control of *all* (that means *everything!*) that takes place. Keep this in mind when Junior crumples a fender on the family car.

In this prayer meeting there was no evidence of disappointment, frustration, or apprehension.

There was no fear of the authorities. (The only fear hinted at in the chapter is the rulers' fear, v. 21, that the public would resent any harm done to the disciples.)

The believers asked God for only one thing for themselves: that they would witness with courage and confidence (cf. v. 29), unintimidated by the dangers that threatened them. For the sake of their witness, they asked that "signs and wonders"—miracles establishing the authenticity of their testimony—would take place in the power of God.

Have you ever been in a prayer meeting like this one? "When they had prayed, the place where they had gathered together was shaken, and they were all filled with the Holy Spirit and began to speak the Word of God with boldness" (v. 31).

Perhaps it is worth noting that there is no evidence that the fullness of the Holy Spirit, here, was accompanied by speaking in tongues (cf. also v. 8). *There is definitely no scriptural basis for insisting that a person is not filled with the Spirit unless he speaks in tongues.*

The fullness of the Spirit, here, was not given for the pleasure of the disciples, so that they might have an ecstatic experience. The Holy Spirit filled them so that they might be better equipped for the service of God and so that they might "speak the Word of God with boldness" (v. 31).

One Life Goal

The great goal of the early Christians was to glorify God. And their faith was more than intellectual. It extended to their hearts and their motives, and it reached into their pocketbooks. They didn't lose sight of the fact that since God had redeemed them, they and all they had belonged to Him.

It's not hard to *say*, "Lord, I am Yours! What do You want me to do?"

It's harder to *live* this way, using what you are and have to the glory of God. We do well to remember that God is not nearly as much concerned with how we would use the $1 million we *don't* have as with what we do with the $10 in our pocket.

Because the early Christians were so generous, "there was not a needy person among them" (v. 34). The fact that this wonderful state of affairs did not last, and that Paul later had to "pass the hat" in Greece for the poor saints in Jerusalem, may indicate misguided zeal, but the principle of our being willing to help a fellow believer in need is valid and timeless.

"All" who had possessions sold them and gave the proceeds to the apostles for redistribution where there was need. Presumably this refers to those who had no resources of their own. Barnabas is mentioned as an example of this kind of generosity.

Their first persecution did not discourage the early Christians, and it is clear that they were really "all out for God."

5
Satan
Attacks

Acts 5

No one likes a hypocrite.

We want the people we deal with to be frank, honest, and on the level. We want to do business with folks we instinctively feel we can trust.

This is especially true in the Church. There is something particularly repelling about someone who merely *pretends* to be a Christian—someone we can't help suspecting is not genuine about his profession of faith in Christ.

Hypocrisy is repulsive to God, too. Because He is holy, sin is highly offensive to Him. Because He is all-knowing, hypocrisy cannot hide from Him. Because He is truth, He hates all pretense and sham.

New Christians were streaming into the Early Church in large numbers, and it was inevitable that before too long the Church should be infiltrated by at least a few "pretenders." Acts 5 records the story of two of them. The inclusion of this unflattering account is evidence of how faithfully the Bible depicts human weaknesses.

The chapter begins with the word "but." In

reading Scripture, it is profitable to stop when one comes to this word and to look for the contrast to which it usually calls attention.

Here the contrast is between Barnabas on the one hand (4:36) and Ananias and Sapphira on the other. Barnabas sold his property and gave the entire proceeds to the apostles. Ananias and Sapphira sold some real estate (BERK) and gave the apostles only *part* of the proceeds.

There was nothing wrong about their retaining some of the money. It was theirs and they could do with it whatever they wished (v. 4). Their sin consisted in *pretending* they were giving God the whole amount.

They were like a person who sings, "I surrender *all*," but who actually is giving the Lord little or nothing. (Or isn't it lying when we sing it?)

They were also like the person who goes to Sunday School, church, and prayer meeting, and who always carries his Bible, but who realizes all too well that he is merely putting on a religious "front" in order to appear "spiritual."

Ananias and Sapphira wanted to play in the same league as Barnabas, but they weren't willing to pay the price.

Putting on a front is dangerous, especially where God is concerned. God knows all there is to know about us. It is a foolish mistake to try to deceive Him.

Putting on a front is foolish where men are concerned, too. Acting as though we are sophisticated or widely traveled or well-read may lead us into painful embarrassment.

Let's determine to be genuine and sincere and honest! Let's ask God to deal with the problems we have previously tried to sidestep through pretense.

The Holy Spirit is able to give us right attitudes if we want Him to.

With God-given insight, Peter at once saw through Ananias' deceit (v. 3) and charged him with lying to the Holy Spirit in his attempt to deceive the Church.

Ananias offered no excuse or explanation. He had no time to do so, for he fell dead as he heard Peter's words.

And his wife, Sapphira, dropped dead a few hours later when she also lied about how much they had received for the property.

The story of Ananias and Sapphira has offended some people. One commentator calls it "frankly repulsive." Even theologians, it seems, take offense at God's judgment on man's sin. St. Augustine thought that, in accordance with Scripture, the lives of this hypocritical couple were taken so that their spirits might be saved in the day of the Lord Jesus (1 Cor. 5:5), but we cannot be certain that Ananias and Sapphira were regenerate. Not *every* member of any group of professed Christians is necessarily a child of God.

Whatever Bible scholars think of the story of Ananias and Sapphira, the event created a sensation in its day. "A strange awe seized the whole church and everybody who heard it" (v. 11, wms).

The public had other reasons for being impressed: "At the hands of the apostles many signs and wonders were taking place among the people" (v. 12).

The early Christians still thought of themselves, probably, as Jews who were worshiping the Messiah. At least, they clung to the Temple (v. 12) as the scene of their religious activity. The Jews still held them in high esteem (v. 13), and multitudes were constantly being added to the number of the believers (v. 14).

Look at the contrast in verse 13: "But none of the rest dared to associate with them." Some Bible scholars believe "the rest" means "the rulers," "the elders," or "the Levites."

Two kinds of people heard the apostles' message and saw the evidences of God at work. The multitudes heard and saw, and many believed. "The rest" were afraid to be swept into this new movement.

Living Dangerously

It was risky, in those days, to become a Christian. One might be put in prison. Worse, one might become unpopular with the "right" people.

Some folks may have shied away from the Church, too, because Christians were living so dangerously. They were getting rid of their possessions. They were spending a great deal of time in the practice of their "religion." They took God and His Word seriously. Telling the Gospel was the most important business in life.

Not everyone "goes" for such a program!

Christians today aren't much like that, are they? We are often so much like the world around us that becoming one of us poses no threat to the potential converts who know us. Becoming a believer, today, little resembles embarking on a new and adventurous way of life.

At least that's the impression we may create.

The Early Church was busy saving souls, but it was also concerned for the poor (4:35) and the sick (5:15, 16). A tremendous healing ministry was being carried on. We aren't told that sick people were actually healed by the shadow of Peter falling across them (v. 15), though that may be implied, but we *are* told that *all* who came were healed.

The apostles exercised the *gift* of healing (Mark 16:18) in those days, and the gift of miracles as well. Many believe that these "sign gifts" are not for the Church today, but let's face the fact that God still heals and He still works miracles. Every redeemed life is a miracle of grace, and multitudes of Christians have seen God answer prayer in many ways—including physical healing.

We can't be sure how much time elapsed between the events recorded in Acts 4 and those narrated in chapter 5, but it may have been a matter of only a few days. The second persecution of the apostles probably came not long behind the first.

This time the high priest in person headed the arrest party (v. 17), along with some of the Sadducees. He put the apostles in jail overnight. When the Holy Spirit is working in power, Christians can expect persecution as well as miracles. And the persecution may well come from the forces of "organized religion." Nothing makes "religious" people more insufferably jealous (v. 17, BERK) than a genuine working of the power of the Holy Spirit which they themselves have not known.

Liberated

An angel let the apostles out of prison in the middle of the night. God can release us, too—from the fetters of sin, bad habits, wrong attitudes, and desperate circumstances. The angel told the apostles to return to the Temple to deliver "the whole message of this Life" (v. 20).

The Gospel is *history*: the birth, death, and resurrection of Jesus Christ. The Gospel is *theology*: regeneration and sanctification and eventual glorification. But we must never lose sight of the fact that being a Christian is more than knowing the facts of history and believing the truths of theology. *It is a way of life.*

It is *the* life. It is God living in us in the person of the Holy Spirit. This is the life that is life indeed (1 Tim. 6:19, ASV).

The angel told the apostles to proclaim this way of life in the Temple. That's where unsaved people were.

It's easy to witness in church before others who share our views. It is much harder in the office before skeptics or on the street before folks who are openly hostile. "The Temple" was where the apostles had been arrested the previous day. They were to return there and take up where they had left off when they were interrupted.

They were back on the job "about daybreak" (v. 21), but many Christians today don't attend Sunday School because they can't get to church an hour before the morning service.

Early Christians were far more rugged. The ministry of the Word held first place in their lives. It had top priority. Daybreak was not too early for them, for they had better things to do than sleep.

A few hours later the high priest convened the Council and the Senate of the Children of Israel (v. 21). He sent officers to the prison to fetch the prisoners.

The officers came back promptly.

"Sir," they reported in some excitement, "we

found the prison locked and in good order, and guards standing at the doors, but when we unlocked the gates and went in, the prisoners weren't there!" (cf. v. 23.)

The court was "perplexed" (v. 24), but not for long! Someone enlightened them: "Those fellows you arrested yesterday? Why, they're back in the Temple, preaching again!"

A few minutes later Peter and his friends had been brought before the religious leaders. The high priest reminded them (v. 28) that this was their second offense. "You are trying to bring this Man's blood on our heads," he said, avoiding the name "Jesus" and the title "Messiah."

Once again, Peter didn't really defend himself, and his remarks were bluntly direct: "*You* put Jesus to death, he told his accusers, but God raised Him from the grave. The One you crucified has been exalted to the right hand of God, a Prince and a Saviour, and in Him there is repentance and forgiveness for Israel" (cf. vv. 30, 31).

Effect of the Gospel

The Gospel causes some men to repent, but it hardens others. The high priest and his cohorts were so furious that they would have killed the apostles at once, but a Pharisee named Gamaliel came to the defense of God's servants.

"Be careful," he warned his associates, after the court had gone into executive session. "If the movement represented by these men is of human origin, it will come to nothing. Remember the insurrection of Theudas and his group? And the rebellion started by Judas of Galilee? Both failed. These men will fail, too, if God isn't on their side. But if

God is *for* them, all your opposition will do no good. You can't fight against God!"

This advice sounded reasonable, and the high priest accepted it. God undoubtedly used Gamaliel to save the lives of the apostles.

But he is no model for you or anyone else to follow! The sort of *neutrality* Gamaliel advised is wrong. Gamaliel should have recognized Messiah's claims and sided with the apostles. He should have embraced Christianity.

But Gamaliel temporized, as so many have done since his day. And God isn't satisfied with compromise. He demands commitment.

Peter and his friends didn't get off scot-free, however. They were flogged before being turned loose with a solemn warning. They rejoiced to be the first to suffer physical pain for Christ's sake.

They had been arrested in the Temple and put in jail the previous afternoon. During the night God's angel had set them free and they had gone back to the Temple at daybreak to preach. The Temple police had picked them up and taken them to face the court, which had them flogged. And when the court released them, where did they go?

Back to the Temple. There, "and from house to house, they kept right on teaching and preaching Jesus as the Christ" (v. 42).

How about us?

Will we *keep right on* witnessing for Christ?

6
Christian Leadership

Acts 6

What happens when someone complains about how the officers of your church are running things?

Do folks put the complainer down as overcritical and instinctively defend the *status quo?* Or do they investigate and fix whatever is wrong, if anything?

Probably it depends on who makes the complaint. Most churches are "blessed" with one or more people who seem to specialize in finding fault. Sometimes their criticisms are ignored even when they are justified.

It wasn't long before the new church in Jerusalem was faced with a complaint. This was at a time when the membership of the church was increasing rapidly and the assembly was suffering growing pains. Methods that once worked fine must often be modified as a church gets larger.

There were now several thousand Christians in Jerusalem. Many were meeting in the Temple, but a growing number of smaller groups were meeting in homes (2:46). (Church buildings were not erected until two or three centuries later.)

As we have seen, some of the Christians had sold at least part of what they owned and given the proceeds to the apostles for distribution to believers who were in need (4:34, 35). Prominent among the latter were widows (6:1), and it would seem that they were being helped under the personal direction of the apostles, possibly in the form of free meals (cf. "serve tables," v. 2).

There were two types of Jews in the Early Church. The Jews who spoke Aramaic and were native to Palestine were called "Hebrews." The others were Hellenistic Jews, spoke Greek, and came from outside of Palestine.

The Hellenists complained that their widows were being overlooked in the daily distribution. There is no mention of discrimination, but it is certainly implied. Why would only Hellenist widows be neglected?

The complaint seems to have been justified. Where there is smoke, there is often fire, and where there is a complaint there is often something wrong. The apostles acted promptly to correct the condition.

The problem, they decided, was that the growing church needed a larger "staff." A staff of one or two persons, adequate in a tiny rural church, cannot carry on effectively in an urban church of a thousand or more.

The apostles called the whole group of Christians together and explained the situation (v. 2). They had studied the problem and were prepared to suggest a remedy, but they looked for and got the approval of the congregation (v. 5) before taking action. They did not merely ask the church to "ratify" something they had already done.

It was not reasonable, the apostles declared,

that they should spend their time serving tables or distributing welfare (v. 2). Their primary responsibility was prayer and the preaching and teaching of the Word of God (v. 4).

The apostles recognized the value of sharing responsibility. A business executive knows how important it is to delegate as much "leg work" as possible in order to free himself for creative thinking and planning. But often the chairman of a church committee spends hours of his time telephoning members or mailing out notices—jobs *any* member of the committee could be doing equally well.

A pastor is a "minister," or servant, of the congregation. His best service is not rendered, however, in running errands for his people, but in praying for and preaching to them. Churches make a tragic mistake when they allow other lesser responsibilities, including purely social ones, to crowd into the time their pastor should have for prayer and the Bible.

Lack of provision, in the average church, for a pastor's own spiritual growth is one reason so many young men, today, are looking for full-time careers in some kind of Christian service *outside* the pastorate.

Notice (v. 4) that "prayer" comes before "the ministry of the Word." Many a pastor who would like to have more time on sermon preparation is satisfied to get along on a prayer life that is utterly inadequate.

(Even if you aren't a pastor, you need to place a high priority on prayer and the Bible. Most Christians pray little, seldom read the Bible, and never *study* it. Result: an anemic, flabby spiritual condition.)

Help Wanted

The apostles' remedy for the situation in the Early Church was for the believers to select seven men to run the church's welfare ministry (v. 3), freeing the apostles from details that had been crowding out time for prayer, study, and preaching.

The seven men who were chosen are sometimes called "deacons." The Greek word from which we get "deacon" means a servant. It applies to the serving of food (v. 1), to waiting on tables (v. 2), and to preaching the Word (v. 4). In a sense, *all of the Christian life* is a *diaconate,* a service, a ministry.

As each organ and member of your physical body contributes its share to the development and welfare of the whole, so each member of the Church, Christ's body, is to contribute to the building up of that spiritual body (Eph. 4:12, 16).

You might think that almost anyone would have qualified to administer welfare—anyone who could ladle soup, carve a roast, and carry a tray. But when "common" tasks are done for Christ they are sanctified and invested with a significance far greater than we ordinarily attach to them.

So it was necessary that these "servants" be well thought of by the group, that they be filled with the Holy Spirit, and that they be men "of good practical sense" (v. 6, wms).

Don't you wonder how a church today would determine whether or not a given individual was filled with the Spirit? A person's reputation is a lot easier to measure than his spirituality!

The Christians chose seven deacons—and there is nothing here about the casting of lots. They brought these men to the apostles, who ordained them by prayer and the laying on of hands. This solemn ceremony symbolized a person's being set apart for some high and holy work.

There is a difference between an apostle and a deacon, and between a church pastor and a church custodian. But we must come back to the awareness that *every* part of God's work is holy and is to be done only by those who are spiritually qualified. Some members, or parts, of the body of Christ seem more "important" than others, but all are necessary. And all are to be highly regarded by the others.

Two of these seven deacons possessed unusual qualifications and went on to larger fields of service. Philip became an evangelist and was responsible for Christianity's penetrating Ethiopia (Acts 8). Stephen (the name, in Greek, means "crown") was a great preacher and became the first Christian to wear a martyr's crown (chap. 7).

A relatively small job is often excellent preparation for bigger responsibilities later. All of us know the "office-boy-to-president" story in the world of business. And there are well-known preachers who first exercised their gifts speaking on street corners, or in personal witnessing.

The ordination of these deacons was the beginning of organization in the Church. Morgan suggests that this chapter shows that Early Church organization was "spiritual, simple, and sufficient." A great deal of subsequent organization, he points out, is "carnal, complex, and corrupt." However, organization is necessary in a church.

Vitality and Growth

Vitality and growth marked the Early Church.

"The Word of God kept on spreading" (v. 7). Its influence went out wherever Christians went, and the disciples "continued to increase *greatly*." This is what one can expect when believers are enthusiastic, rather than apathetic, about their faith, and when Christianity is a way of life rather than a set of religious formalities.

Even "a great many" of the priests came to believe. Some may have been converted in the Temple, but the only way to explain the continuing phenomenal growth of the Church is that individual believers witnessed actively wherever they went, and brought new converts into the Christian groups to which they belonged. Obviously the apostles did not do *all* the evangelizing.

Stephen, one of the seven table-servers, was a man who not only did the job given him, but looked for additional opportunities to put his gifts to work. He was the sort of person God can use in many ways. "Full of grace and power" (v. 8), he exercised the gifts of miracles and of healing, and his work in the Church was so outstanding that he was singled out for attack by the enemies of the faith.

These opponents argued with Stephen but were "unable to cope with the wisdom and the Spirit with which he was speaking" (v. 10).

There is an adage, "If you can't win the argument, start a fight." Stephen's foes, unable to controvert his preaching, decided on a "smear" campaign to get rid of him. Like Queen Jezebel, who hired perjurers to accuse Naboth falsely so that he might be put to death (1 Kings 21), these men falsely accused Stephen of blaspheming Moses and Jehovah. Even Christian Jews held Moses in highest regard, and this lying charge enlisted antagonism to Stephen among "the people" (Acts 6: 12).

Up to this time, the Christians had been held in high general esteem (2:47; 5:13). This incident marks the beginning of public resistance and opposition to God's people.

Stephen had no doubt preached the superiority of the Jesus way over Judaism. He had probably declared that God could be worshiped anywhere rather than only at the Temple. He had no doubt contrasted the liberty of grace with the bondage of Law. His enemies twisted his words (vv. 13, 14) and accused him of blasphemy on the basis of lying testimony.

As a result of these trumped-up charges by men who were no match for him in logic, Stephen was taken before the Sanhedrin.

There is a tremendously important warning here for all of us:

Don't believe everything you hear about people.

Successful men, in business, in politics, and in the Church, are likely to be victims of smear campaigns.

When people are jealous of a person, they don't always feel it necessary to stick to the truth.

A young pastor just out of a leading evangelical seminary had been preaching only a few years when a group of disgruntled members left his church. Not long afterward friends of his, talking to people in another evangelical church in the city, were appalled to hear this young man denounced as "liberal" in his theology. The "evidence" for this serious charge was that

• he did not preach from the King James Version of the Bible;

• he did not put enough emphasis on Christ's

second coming; and
* he did not give altar calls.

Not one of these practices, obviously, is any indication of "liberal" theology.

When you hear some Christian being condemned, wait a minute! Don't be too quick to believe all you hear. Sometimes lies are circulated out of malicious spite. Sometimes they start out as truths but get distorted as they are passed from eager gossip to eager gossip.

Stephen was put to death on the basis of a series of misrepresentations. Since his time, many a man has lost his good reputation in the same way. The hearts of God's faithful servants have been broken and their ministry hindered by the circulation, innocently or otherwise, of untruths.

Stephen's face was like the face of an angel when he faced his accusers (v. 15). One would think that even his heartless critics could have known that the man who stood before them, full of the Holy Spirit, *must* have been innocent of the terrible charges against him.

Maybe the Sanhedrin *knew*, but they were not going to be put off. It was time for overt action against this new cult that was upsetting Jerusalem and threatening the religious leaders and their comfortable way of life.

Determined to proceed, they demanded of Stephen whether or not he pleaded guilty to the charges (7:1).

7
Resisting Change

Acts 7

A generation or two ago it was not uncommon for a family to live in the same house for a whole lifetime. Today this may be true of some, especially in rural areas, but the average American family moves once every five years or oftener.

Frequent moving is only one item on a long list of changes that are taking place in America. Our ways of traveling, the kind of homes we build, our reading habits, our use of radio and TV, the food we buy and the places where we buy it—all these have changed and are still changing rapidly. Even the style of men's clothes, whether or not they like it, is changing dramatically from year to year.

In his best-selling book, *Future Shock,* first published in 1970, Alvin Toffler deals with the problems created by today's rapid changes. Physiologically, emotionally, and otherwise, man is not designed to endure changes at so rapid a rate, and Toffler says he may not survive his "collision with tomorrow."

Many of us are reluctant to accept change. We would prefer to go on living in the way to which we have become accustomed. We talk a lot about "the good old days." But change is inevitable, and accept it we must. On some remote island we might escape it, but few of us are in a position to move to such a refuge.

Young people, however, often welcome change. Sometimes they seem to want it for its own sake. They tell us that our culture is in such bad shape that *any* change would be an improvement.

Obviously, change is desirable *only* if it improves the state of affairs.

In the Church, as you would expect, change is especially controversial.

Many Christians, especially younger believers, are afraid the Church has become stagnant and unproductive and that it ought to adopt new ways of doing God's work.

Some older believers object strongly to any such idea. God, they say, is changeless and unchanging. He works in the same way today as He did in the first century. When their church changes its way of doing things, such believers feel threatened.

God in History

Stephen's accusers had no evidence on which to indict him, so they hired false witnesses who charged him with blasphemy (Acts 6:13, 14).

"Are these things so?" the high priest asked him (7:1).

Stephen did not really answer this question. He did not defend himself. What he proceeded to say was calculated to arouse, rather than pacify, his accusers. In fact, they became so infuriated that he had no chance to finish his address.

Stephen's message is a summary of Israel's history. Probably this chapter gives us only a short summary of an address that lasted at least an hour or more.

• First Stephen called attention to the truth that God is not limited to any geographical area. The Jews liked to think that special blessing attached to Palestine's holy soil. This may once have been true, but not since Pentecost. Palestine is no closer to heaven today than Hoboken, New Jersey.

Even in the days of the patriarchs, Stephen pointed out, God also spoke to men in Ur of the Chaldees and in Haran of Mesopotamia (7:2). He saw, was with, and delivered His people when they were in Egypt. He spoke to Moses at the burning bush on the Sinai peninsula.

In a day when each nation claimed its own private deity, Stephen was telling his hearers that it isn't necessary to be in any certain part of the world to hear and to serve the Creator.

• Stephen's second point was that the patriarchs obeyed God. Abraham, though he had no idea where he was going, obediently left Chaldea and went to Haran. Later he moved to Canaan. He believed God was giving the Land of Canaan to his descendants, though he then had no children and though as long as he lived he owned no more of Canaan than a cemetery lot (Gen. 23).

Jacob, too, obeyed God, sending his sons to Egypt for grain which was available because God had previously sent Joseph, Jacob's son, to interpret Pharaoh's dream and become head of the Egyptian Department of Welfare and Grain Sales.

Moses obeyed God. Brought up in the splendor of the Egyptian court, he felt the Lord calling him to help his people. He answered the call prematurely, but after he had spent 40 years in the desert he was completely prepared. And when God spoke to him at the burning bush, he went and did as the Lord told him.

• The third truth that Stephen drove home to his accusers was that though the patriarchs had obeyed God even when they did not fully understand what He was doing, the people of Israel, on the whole, were rebellious and disobedient.

This tendency was evident in how Joseph's brothers treated him, selling him into slavery in Egypt.

Then there was Moses. The Jews of the first century had an extremely lofty opinion of Moses. The people of Israel had rejected Moses, however, when he wanted to become their deliverer (Acts 7:24-25). They misunderstood him and threatened him, forcing him to flee the country and hide in the Midian desert for 40 years.

Even after God had delivered the Israelites from their bondage, leading them through the Red Sea on dry land, Moses' experience with them in the wilderness was one long series of complaints and rebellions. They "were unwilling to be obedient to him, but repudiated him and in their hearts turned back to Egypt" (v. 39).

The high point in the people's rebellion was when they had Aaron make a golden calf for them to worship, and when they planned to go back to Egypt without Moses (vv. 40, 41).

Another high point, not mentioned by Stephen, was the people's refusal, at Kadesh-barnea, to enter Canaan. As a result they had to spend another 40 years in the wilderness. There they took up with one form of idolatry after another (vv. 42, 43).

Chronic Griping

Stephen clearly demonstrated that Israel's history had been marked by grumbling against God's will and frequent rebellion against Him and His servants, their leaders.

It was especially noteworthy that the people had rebelled so insistently against Moses, for it was Moses who had promised that God would send them a Prophet like himself (v. 37). This Prophet, of course, was the Lord Jesus. But when He came, He received the same treatment the people had given Moses.

• Stephen went on to his fourth and most explosive point. By this time his judges saw what he was driving at, and we may be sure they were sitting on the edges of their seats.

Stephen began this part of his speech by reminding his hearers of the tabernacle in the wilderness (v. 44), where the Ark, symbolizing God's presence, was housed and where God's people were to bring their offerings and worship Him.

Some commentators believe Stephen implied plainly that since the Tabernacle preceded the Temple, and since it was specifically designed by God, it was even a more ideal place for the worship of Jehovah than the Temple. According to this view, the Temple, which God *allowed* Solomon to build, was a secondary place for God's worship. A portable tent is seen as far more appropriate than a permanent building for the worship of a God who may be approached anywhere.

This very idea was a hard blow to Stephen's hearers, who venerated the Temple.

Stephen did not stop here, however. He went on to state flatly that "the Most High does not dwell in houses made by human hands" (v. 48). He quoted Old Testament Scriptures to prove this— an assertion which would startle men who conceived of God as actually dwelling between the cherubim of the Ark.

Stephen had showed his hearers that God isn't "in a rut." His ways of working with men are subject to variation. There was development and progress, during Israel's history, in God's dealings with His people.

The Sanhedrin had grown restless as Stephen spoke. They resented his references to rebellion and murmuring among the Jews. And when he began to reflect on the Temple, the most cherished of their institutions and the source of their affluence and prestige, they could stand him no longer.

Sensing that his hearers were about to cut him off, Stephen brought his "defense" to an early and abrupt end. Disregarding his planned conclusion, he charged the Sanhedrin with the same obstinacy as had characterized their ancestors (v. 51). Their forefathers had persecuted and killed the prophets, and they themselves had betrayed and murdered the Righteous One whom the prophets had foretold (v. 52). They had boasted about the Law, given as it was by angels, but had not obeyed it (v. 53).

Found Guilty

A supernatural touch had attended the beginning of Stephen's "trial," when the members of the Council had noticed that his face resembled the face of an angel (6:15). As his judges gnashed their teeth in rage at the implications of his words, Stephen had a glimpse of Christ in glory, and openly told his accusers what he saw (7:55, 56). This revelation only infuriated them the more. Cut to the quick, they covered their ears to shut out the "blasphemy," and hurried him out of the city lest its holiness be defiled by his blood. They stoned him outside the walls as he called on Jesus to receive his spirit.

The Sanhedrin could not legally execute anyone without the approval of the Roman procurator, Pontius Pilate. Pilate was out of the city at this time, but historians suppose that he was only too willing to look the other way on such occasions as this, in the interests of keeping Rome's uneasy peace with the Jews.

Stephen became the first Christian martyr. He was not a martyr simply because he died for his faith; he died because he was a martyr. The Greek word *marturion,* from which "martyr" comes, means "witness." The martyrs were witnesses who sealed their testimony with their blood.

Stephen's accusers put him to death because they could not tolerate his message. His new doctrine, which we call Christianity, implied that God is living, vital, dynamic, and progressive. Their God was static and inert.

It is true that God Himself is beyond change. He is always the same. It is also a fact that *truth* does not change. Doctrines that were true in Jesus' day are just as valid today. Anyone who adds to or subtracts from the Word of God brings a curse on himself (Rev. 22:18, 19).

But we must distinguish between the plain teachings of Scripture and the interpretations of men. We must not be slaves to *tradition*—to *man's* ways of doing God's work.

For instance, some Christians get upset if a

church changes its order of worship. Or they resent the appearance at their services of young men with long hair and bare feet. They object to the use of any version of Scripture other than the one they have always read—even if their favorite version doesn't communicate well to most people today. They condemn church members who like to meet in homes for Bible study, sharing, and prayer instead of being in church on Wednesday evening. They can't stand use of a kind of church music foreign to what they are accustomed to, even if young people respond to it.

In short, they seem to look at any new way of doing things as a threat.

Such people could learn from Stephen. God is alive; He is active; He isn't limited to the ways of working that men set up for Him.

One test of the methods we use in doing God's work is, "Are they *right?*" But another tests is, "Are they producing results? Are people being saved? Are lives being changed?" If the answers are "No," we had better ask "Why not?"

Sin may be responsible.

But then again, maybe we resemble the Jewish leaders to whom Stephen spoke. They didn't grasp what he was telling them. A great break was coming between Judaism and the Gospel. The Temple and Jewish worship were like old wineskins. They could no longer contain the strong new wine of the Gospel. A new day was dawning, and it called for a new approach.

If we are going to penetrate today's culture effectively, perhaps we need to be willing to try new ways—not because they are *different* but because people are responding to them.

The alternative is for us to stay in our comfortable ruts. If unsaved people want salvation badly enough, they'll come under *our* conditions.

Let's face the fact that people today aren't what people were 50 years ago, or even 25 years ago. They are still sinners, to be sure; they still need salvation. But their ways of thinking, after long exposure to modern science and technology, are quite different from what they were a generation back.

The Church has the same message today that it had in Stephen's time, but we need to present it in such a way that people will listen.

You just can't get attention for the Gospel today as easily as you could before the days of radio, TV, movies, and other mass media.

Here and there, pastors and youth workers with creativity are using new approaches that are gaining a hearing for the truth. Laymen are being trained to do the work of evangelists and the Gospel is reaching the public, through laymen, out where the public is.

And often the Christians doing these things are roundly criticized as "liberal" by older believers who are wedded to tradition.

But should we oppose those who see the need for change and are actively doing what they can to reach today's unbelievers with the message of God's love?

Should we insist that God stay in our rut?

8
Apostle
vs.
Magician

Acts 8

If someone shows you two eggs, one raw and the other hardboiled, can you tell them apart? They look and feel exactly alike. But just lay them on a table and spin them. The boiled egg spins readily; the raw egg spins reluctantly.

If you know how, you can tell the difference between a raw egg and a boiled one.

Telling the difference between a professing Christian and a genuine believer is somewhat more difficult, but God can do it. Men get into *a* church without being reborn, but they don't get into *the* Church. They don't get into the body of Christ.

Acts 9 deals with two "converts" to the Early Church. One was genuine, the other was a phony. The account is interesting and instructive.

Four or five years had elapsed since Pentecost. The Christians were now a sizable group, numbering perhaps 10,000 or more, and though they doubtless had occasional scrapes with the Jewish religious leaders, life in Jerusalem was not too unpleasant for them.

But they had settled down.

They remembered that they were to be Christ's witnesses in Jerusalem, but they apparently overlooked the rest of the command: ". . . and in all Judea and Samaria, and even to the uttermost part of the earth" (Acts 1:8).

God had to remind them.

The day that his grieving friends buried Stephen, a man named Saul, who had wholeheartedly concurred in Stephen's execution, started a full-scale persecution of members of the new Church. As a result, believers began to leave Jerusalem. And as they went, they preached the Word (8:4). Only the apostles remained in the city to direct the Church. Those in leadership positions must sometimes expose themselves to greater risks than rank-and-file workers.

The hero of Acts 8 is Philip (v. 5), one of the seven table-servers appointed to distribute relief to widows (6:5).

When Philip left Jerusalem he went to Samaria and began preaching Christ there. This was in itself unusual, for customarily Jews had no dealings with Samaritans (John 4:9). They despised the Samaritans, who originated centuries earlier when Jews intermarried with heathen people (2 Kings 17).

Philip knew that God loves all mankind (John 3:16), including Samaritans. God's love goes out to Jew and Gentile, black and white, rich and poor, high and low.

Philip's preaching was accompanied by mighty miracles (Acts 8:6). He exorcised unclean spirits and healed those who were lame, paralyzed, and sick. The people who listened to him could not help being convinced that he spoke in the power of God, and many trusted Christ as Saviour.

Mock Conversion

One of Philip's professed converts was a magician by the name of Simon. This man had claimed to be "the Word of God, the Comforter, the Almighty, and all there is of God." He was more than a conceited magician; he was a blaspheming servant of Satan whom the devil was using in an effort to stop the spread of the Gospel into Samaria.

Satan never bothers a "dead" church or a "dead" Christian. Why should he? Only those actively serving God deserve—or require—his opposition.

Simon had a big following. "Everybody, high and low, kept running after him" (v. 10, wms). Those were restless, unsettled days. People were hungry for peace of mind and heart, and they turned to cults and isms very much as people today are embracing astrology, witchcraft, and Satanism in their frantic effort to find the satisfaction available only in Christ.

The fact that Simon "believed" (v. 13) does not necessarily mean that he exercised saving faith. "He was simply convinced of the potency of the name of Jesus when he saw the mighty works wrought by its means" (Bruce).

Simon was compelled to admit that the miracles Philip performed were genuine. He assented mentally to what Philip preached—he admitted that Philip spoke the truth (cf. James 2:19). His later actions, however, give us no reason for believing that Simon was born again.

Simon was baptized, but no one is saved by submitting to this ceremony. No amount of water, of itself, will make anyone right with God.

No doubt Philip believed, when he baptized Simon, that the sorcerer was honest in his profession of faith, but Philip could not see into Simon's heart. He did not need to. Jesus says that the Church is like a net in which good fish and bad are caught. In the day of judgment, God will sort out the good from the bad (Matt. 13:47-50).

Apostles Investigate

When news of the Samaritan revival reached Jerusalem, Peter and John went to see for themselves how the Gospel was spreading. They found that the new converts had not yet received the Holy Spirit (v. 16). When they laid hands on them, the Spirit fell upon them.

Another delayed receiving of the Spirit is mentioned later (19:2), but a study of The Acts shows that *usually* the Holy Spirit came upon men without the laying on of hands. *Christians receive the Spirit when they put their trust in Christ.* It is the Spirit who baptizes them into the Church, the body of Christ (1 Cor. 12:13).

One explanation for this event in Samaria is that the receiving of the Holy Spirit was delayed until the arrival of Peter and John so that the apostles themselves might have a share in the Samaritan ministry. Relations between the Jews and the Samaritans had long been strained, to put it mildly, and if the apostles had not been plainly linked with the Samaritan revival, the age-old rivalry might have been perpetuated and *two* Christian churches might have come into being.

In any case, remember that The Acts is a book of history, not doctrine. God's teaching on the Holy Spirit is plainly given in the New Testament epistles.

When Simon saw the apostles impart the Spirit

through the laying on of hands, he was eager to acquire this ability for himself. He offered to pay for it (v. 18), and his action has given our language the term "simony"—an attempt to turn spiritual functions into marketable commodities.

People who think the size of their contributions to a church entitles them to positions of influence or authority come close to being guilty of this sin.

"May your money go to perdition with you, because you thought you could buy the gift of God for money; you have neither share nor part of this message, for your heart is not right in God's sight" (vv. 20, 21, BERK), said Peter, calling on Simon to repent. "For I see," Peter concluded, "that you are a bitter weed and a bundle of crookedness!" (v. 23, WMS).

Simon wanted to escape the consequences of his sin (v. 24) more than he wanted to get right with God, and there is no record of his ever repenting. Tradition says he viciously opposed the Apostle Peter for years, that he was worshiped in Rome, and that he founded a sect called the Simonians. In an effort to perform one last miracle, he had his followers bury him alive for three days, but when they opened the grave he was dead. He has been called "the father of all heresies."

Genuine Conversion

Peter and John returned to Jerusalem, preaching in Samaritan villages along their route, but an angel told Philip to go south to the Gaza Road, which traversed the desert and led to Egypt.

How would you have felt, had you been Philip? Can't you imagine his saying, "But, Angel, what is there to *go* to down there? Nothing but desert! Wouldn't it be wiser for me to wait here at least till this revival slows down?"

But Philip didn't reason with the angel. He simply obeyed, and therefore he was part of one of the most remarkable "coincidences" of all time.

On the Gaza road he saw the chariot of a VIP, probably accompanied by guards and attendants. The passenger in the main vehicle was reading a scroll of the Prophet Isaiah. Possession of such a scroll was in itself an indication that this was a person of more than ordinary consequence.

What do *you* read when you travel? It's seldom that one sees an itinerant businessman or public official (this chariotrider was treasurer of Ethiopia!) reading the Bible!

Urged on by the Holy Spirit (v. 29), Philip ran alongside the Ethiopian's chariot and heard him reading aloud from Isaiah 53. The Lord had so guided all the circumstances that at the moment of Philip's arrival the Ethiopian was at the precise part of Isaiah that would give Philip a wonderful opening for a clear testimony to the Saviour!

"Do you understand what you're reading?" asked Philip politely (v. 30).

"Well, how could I unless someone guides me?" asked the Ethiopian, moving over on the chariot seat and inviting Philip aboard (v. 31).

It wasn't long before the treasurer was no longer ignorant about the crucified Saviour.

Philip must have said something about baptism, for when they came to "some water," the new Christian asked to be baptized.

Verse 37 isn't in the best manuscripts, but Irenaeus, one of the Church Fathers, quoted it in the second century, before the date of the oldest existing New Testament manuscript. It probably tells what happened, for the verse reflects the baptismal practice of the Early Church.

After Philip had baptized the Ethiopian, his work for God on the Gaza road was finished, and the Holy Spirit "snatched" Philip away. The same term is used of the Rapture of the Church, and it indicates a miraculous departure.

The Ethiopian went on his way rejoicing (v. 39), a new creature in Christ. He experienced the same kind of joy that had prevailed in Samaria (v. 8) while Philip had been preaching there.

How much joy do we perhaps miss by failing to witness? Not every Christian can be an evangelist, but no one is denied the privilege of telling people about the Lord Jesus and His power to save.

As for Philip, he "found himself at Azotus [a town about 10 miles north of Gaza]; and as he passed through he kept preaching the Gospel to all the cities until he came to Caesarea" (v. 40).

Philip seems to have adopted Caesarea as his headquarters and to have continued serving the Lord there as an evangelist. Some 20 years later, when the Apostle Paul visited him, he had four daughters, all of whom had the gift of prophecy (21:8, 9).

Tradition tells us that the Ethiopian treasurer returned to his native land and planted the seeds of Christianity there. His queen, it is said, was one of his first converts. Unfortunately, it was centuries before the Scriptures were available to the Ethiopian Christians in their own language. As a result, the Coptic Church, the branch of Christianity that developed there, is twisted and perverted. It is impossible to overemphasize how important it is for people to have the Word of God in their own language. Thank God for the heroic efforts being made to put the Bible into every living language in the world today, including into English *as it is spoken now.*

What was the difference between the conversion of Simon the Magician and that of the Ethiopian treasurer?

The difference between them is the difference between any person who is only superficially "converted" and one who is genuinely born again.

Simon believed Philip's miracles were genuine. He believed that the message Philip proclaimed was true. He gave mental assent to the Gospel.

He was like people today who think that if they believe that Jesus is the Son of God and that He died for sinners and rose again, they are Christians.

But though New Testament faith *includes* intellectual acceptance of a set of doctrines, it is much more. It is a matter of a person's committing himself to the One at the center of these doctrines. It involves admitting one's personal need and personally trusting Christ for forgiveness and new life. It includes giving oneself over to Him so that His Spirit may possess one and control one's life.

Paul suggests that it is well to check whether or not one is in the faith (2 Cor. 13:5). It is not at all necessary to *wonder* whether we are regenerate. It is possible for us to *know* for certain that we are children of God (1 John 5:13).

9
Struck Down by Christ

Acts 9

The conversion of Saul of Tarsus, otherwise known as the Apostle Paul, was such an unlikely event, thought a British agnostic of the last century, that it should not be difficult to disprove. In so doing he could show the rest of the New Testament unworthy of credibility also. This would undermine the whole foundation of the Christian faith.

So George Lord Lyttleton went to work to show how impossible it would have been for a man like Saul to have changed the direction of his life so diametrically. It was obvious, he thought, that Saul was putting on an act, *pretending* to have been converted.

Lyttleton put the results of his study into a book, *Observations on the Conversion and Apostleship of Saint Paul.* His amazing conclusion? "Paul's conversion and apostleship alone, duly considered, are a demonstration sufficient to prove Christianity to be a divine revelation."

As a result of his research, Lyttleton himself trusted Christ as his personal Saviour.

That the evangelist Luke considered Saul's conversion to be of critical importance is evident. In the limited space at his disposal in The Acts he narrates this incident, in detail, three times (chaps. 9, 22, 26).

A Roman citizen of Tarsus, in Asia Minor, Saul was brought up after the strictest Hebrew tradition. He had an excellent education and was what some might call "an intellectual." He was thoroughly familiar with the Old Testament and related Hebrew documents.

When the Sanhedrin stoned Stephen, Saul approved wholeheartedly. He used that occasion to launch a full-scale persecution of the new Church, hauling converts, both men and women, off to prison (8:3). He even got extradition papers from the high priest (9:2) and set out for Damascus, 140 miles from Jerusalem, to arrest Christians there and bring them back to Jerusalem for possible torture and execution.

Saul was undoubtedly sincere in all he did. He is a conspicuous example of the truth that a person who is sincerely wrong is still wrong in spite of all his sincerity.

The city of Damascus was already ancient in the time of Abraham. Saul, traveling with a group, had almost reached it—some traditions say he was only a quarter of a mile from the gate—when a bright light from heaven shone around him.

All sorts of inadequate explanations have been offered to explain away what Luke says took place. Some say the bright light was the dazzling reflection of the noonday sun on the white buildings of Damascus. Some dismiss the appearance of Christ to Saul as "a subjective experience." One scholar says that Saul had been thinking about Christ for weeks, and that "the light" now dawned on him and changed his mind.

"It has been urged," A. T. Robertson writes, "that Paul had an epileptic fit, that he had a sunstroke, that he fell off his horse to the ground, that he had a nightmare, that he was blinded by a flash of lightning, that he imagined he saw Jesus as a result of his highly wrought nervous state, or that he deliberately renounced Judaism because of a growing conviction that the disciples were right. But the conversion of Paul cannot be accounted for except by Paul's own interpretation of the change it made in him. *He saw Jesus and surrendered to Him.*"

Personal Encounter

A personal encounter with Christ is always at the beginning of the Christian life. Such an encounter is no less real for being much less spectacular than Saul's. Few Christians have visions or see lights when they come to Christ. They may have no special feelings about the experience. But they know they have responded to Christ's invitation, "Come unto Me," and that they believe His promise to forgive them and make them new. Saving faith is taking God at His word and believing that He honors the commitment you make.

When the heavenly light flashed around Saul, he fell to the ground (though not necessarily from a horse) and heard a voice asking, "Saul, Saul, why are you persecuting Me?" (v. 4).

Sometimes faith in Christ is preceded by a time during which a person is led gradually to a transforming experience with God, but salvation itself is always instantaneous. One may be *near* the moment of salvation or *far* from it, but one is never half saved and at the same time half lost.

"Who are You, Sir?" asked Saul in response to the voice. (This is an accepted translation, for the word "lord" is used either of deity or as a term of human address; e.g., Luke 12:36, av. Many believe that Saul did not know *who* had addressed him.)

"I am Jesus, whom you are persecuting," said the risen Lord (v. 5).

In what sense was Saul persecuting Jesus? Each believer is part of Christ's body. When a part of the body suffers, the Head suffers, too (cf. 1 Cor. 12:26; Matt. 25:35-45). Thus, Saul's persecution of Christians was a persecution of Jesus. We ought to remember this, especially when we are tempted to snub, criticize, condemn, oppose, or speak against any of God's people.

A wave of regret must have flooded Saul's mind when he recognized the enormity of his past actions. Earnestly and sincerely thinking that he had been opposing God's enemies, he had actually been attacking God's own Son!

But Saul was a straightforward, practical individual. He knew that the past could not be undone. His concern was with the present and the future, over which he had a measure of control. So he asked, "Lord [and here he used the term as an indication of Christ's deity], what will You have me to do?"

(It is true that these words are not in the best manuscripts of Acts 9, but they record what Saul actually said. They are unquestioned where they occur in chapter 22.)

Many Christian lives are unproductive because Christians sometimes fail for years to ask God, What will You have me to do? Saul asked for instructions *immediately* upon his conversion. Some believers *never* get around to asking.

How about *you*? Do you *know* what God wants you to be doing? Are you *doing* it?

Saul was temporarily blinded by his vision. His associates led him into Damascus, where the Lord had told him (v. 6) he would be given further directions. There, after three days of blindness, fasting, and prayer, he was visited by a disciple named Ananias. Sent to Saul by God, Ananias laid his hands on the new convert and baptized him. Saul regained his vision and was filled with the Holy Spirit.

The Lord had told Ananias that Saul was a "chosen instrument" (v. 15) to take the name of Jesus "to Gentiles and kings and the Children of Israel.

Even though God revealed to Saul "how much he must suffer for My name's sake," this new convert was not reluctant to accept his assignment. A career of Christian service, "full-time" or not, almost guarantees one will meet with ridicule, resistance, or even hatred. Early Christians were happy that they were allowed to suffer with and for their Lord Jesus (5:41).

It's not likely that God showed Saul all his future sufferings in some kind of visionary preview. He more likely made it clear, step by step, that tribulations for Christ's sake were to be his lot. "Paul's road, from Damascus to Rome," says Woodbridge, "was stained with blood and tears."

The apostle wasted no time getting to work. He went from one Damascus synagogue to another preaching Jesus. Many a new Christian with Saul's supernatural experience would have spent most of his life giving his personal testimony. Saul felt free to tell his experience, but almost always he preached that Jesus was the Christ, the Son of God (v. 20).

You can imagine how the Damascus Jews reacted to this preaching from the man who had come all the way from Jerusalem to punish Christians!

In the Desert

We know from Galatians 1:16, 17 that Saul did not stay long in Damascus. He went to the desert of Arabia, there to be alone with the Lord. That time was to him what the 40 years in the back side of the desert were to Moses. Both these men needed solitude, time to think, and time for communion with God. During the time Saul spent in the desert, the Lord undoubtedly gave him many of the revelations embodied in his epistles, which form a substantial part of the New Testament.

After Saul's return from Arabia, Damascus soon got too hot for him, and he had to flee to save his life. Such a retreat is not always evidence of cowardice—it may well be discretion, the better part of valor. "A live dog is better than a dead lion" (Ecc. 9:4). God had scheduled too much work for Saul for him to be martyred just yet!

Saul's escape from Damascus was not exactly glorious. His friends let him down over the city wall in a hamper, or basket!

Saul's greatest obstacle in the Church, at this time, was his own past. The Jerusalem Christians refused to believe his claims of conversion. He was in the position of a man just out of prison after serving a long term. No employer will hire him because of his past mistakes and criminal record.

All of us make mistakes, do foolish things, and sin. As we repent, God graciously forgives us and forgets our past. But men are not always ready to forget, and it may take a Christian a long time to live down wasted years or even a moment of folly or a few careless words.

The Lord had used Ananias in Damascus to befriend Saul, instruct him, and introduce him to the Christian community. In Jerusalem, He used Barnabas (v. 27; cf. 4:36), who came to Saul's assistance, sponsored him, and told the believers about this new Christian's dramatic conversion.

Are there new believers around us who need us to play an Ananias or Barnabas role?

After Barnabas had spoken for Saul, the latter "was one of them" (v. 28, wey).

Saul was eager to witness to his former associates, the Jewish religious and intellectual leaders, with whom he had so savagely persecuted the Christians. He wanted to tell them the Good News about Christ, so that they too might come into a right relationship with God through His Son.

But the Jews were not as anxious to hear Saul's testimony as he had thought they would be. He continued to preach boldly—not bluntly and boorishly, but positively and aggressively—but he could not break down their animosity. "They kept trying to murder him" (v. 29, wms).

Finally the other believers, perhaps sensing that Saul was an unusually gifted individual and that God had a tremendous task ahead for him, decided that Jerusalem was too "hot" for him. They took him to Caesarea and put him on a ship sailing to Tarsus, his native city. He probably remained there for three or four years, during which time the Lord further equipped him for the great work he would do.

Job Opportunities

"So the Church throughout all Judea and Galilee and Samaria enjoyed peace, being built up; and, going on in the fear of the Lord and in the comfort of the Holy Spirit, it continued to increase" (v. 31).

The first word of verse 31, "so," implies that the result described here was due to factors mentioned in the preceding verses. As Bruce says, "The first wave of persecution seems to have died down with the conversion of the leading persecutor."

The Church had a measure of peace, but it didn't last long. More important, the Church was "built up," and its followers continued to increase in number.

Chapter 9 closes with another reference to the work of Simon Peter, the most often mentioned person in the first 12 chapters of the book. He seems to have had a sort of itinerant ministry, "going here and there" (v. 32, WMS). Two of his miracles are mentioned here, one at Lydda and another at Joppa, but probably there were many others. As was often the case, such miracles won a hearing for the Gospel, and many people were saved through Peter's preaching.

As you reflect on the events recorded in Acts 9, you may wish that your conversion had been as dramatic and revolutionary as that of Saul.

A dramatic conversion is good material for an interesting personal testimony, and unusual conversions still happen, though they are in the minority. Most people come to Christ without a vision, a miraculous light, and three days of blindness.

Instead of hankering for a conversion experience like Saul's, why not try for the experience of Ananias or Barnabas? These were the men who befriended Saul shortly after he became a believer.

Christians ought to watch for opportunities to befriend others. Visitors in church, new converts, new members—all need special attention. Unless we make them feel welcome, take them to our hearts and into our homes, and demonstrate in our words and actions that we care about them, they may conclude that there is no real place for them in our church.

Often we respond warmly to new Christians who have pleasant personalities, unusual talents, good reputations, or better-than-average financial means. These are the very persons who least need our help. We tend to leave other new Christians, or newcomers to our church, to shift more or less for themselves.

Another person whom more of us could imitate with profit to our church is Tabitha, or Dorcas, the godly woman who was known for her simple works of practical charity. There are no apostles today, but the Lord could use many Barnabasses and Dorcases in His Church!

Any takers?

10
Reaching Out
Acts 10 and 11

A "society" church in a prosperous midwestern city, having received a substantial legacy, was planning to rebuild. The members were asked by the board of trustees to choose between a large, unpretentious edifice and a small, elegant one. They decided on the small, elegant one.

"We appeal only to the more prosperous element in the community," explained one of the elders, "and so we will probably have a small congregation."

Few churches are as openly snobbish as this one, but discrimination is present, unhappily, in a large number of Christian congregations.

When Philip went to preach to the Samaritans (Acts 8), he took the first step toward recognizing that God wants *all* men to hear the Gospel message.

The Samaritans were mixed-blood descendants of the Hebrews left in Palestine when others of the ten tribes of the Northern Kingdom were carried off by the Assyrians (722 B.C.). The people left behind had intermarried with the pagan Canaanites and immigrants, and the Jews despised the Samaritans for this mixed Jewish-heathen ancestry. The Samaritans worshiped Jehovah but accepted only the Pentateuch, the first five books of the Bible.

Momentous Decision

In Acts 10 and 11 we find the record of how the Christian Church reached a monumental decision. These chapters tell how the Gospel got started on its way to the far places of earth. Here we learn what kept Christianity from becoming merely a variation of Judaism. It is hard to overestimate the importance of the new trend that began in the Church at this time.

Some six years had probably elapsed since Stephen's death and the initial persecution of Christians in Jerusalem. As the believers fled the city to avoid oppression, they preached the Gospel—but *they preached only to Jews* (11:19). Apparently it never occurred to these Hebrew believers that God had much interest in anyone but Jews! This attitude came easily, for they had been accustomed to believe that Jews had a sort of monopoly on Jehovah, the true God. They seem to have interpreted the Great Commission (Matt. 28:19, 20) and Jesus' final command (Acts 1:8) solely in terms of their own ethnic group.

Though Paul is called "the apostle to the Gentiles," it was through Peter that God first revealed the great truth that the message about Christ is for *all* men, Jews or Gentiles.

Peter was at Joppa at the home of Simon the tanner. While he was in prayer on the flat roof of the house, he had a vision of a sheet being lowered out of heaven, full of animals both clean and unclean. ("Clean" animals were those which the Jews were allowed to eat.) Peter heard a voice say, "Arise, Peter, kill and eat!"

"But Lord," replied Peter, in effect, "I never eat anything that isn't kosher!"

"What God has cleansed," said the Lord, "no longer consider unholy" (v. 15).

Peter had this vision three times.

While the apostle was wondering what it all meant, a delegation of Gentiles from Caesarea came to the door of Simon's house and asked for Peter. The Holy Spirit told him that he should go with these men, and of course he obeyed.

The men took Peter to the home of Cornelius, a captain in the Roman army attached to what was called the Italian Cohort.

A few days earlier, Cornelius had also been in prayer (10:1-4). Mutual prayer was responsible for Peter and Cornelius getting together. (Is your prayer life strong enough so that God can use it to give you direction and wisdom?)

Cornelius was a moral man, generous to the poor, who feared God and was faithful in prayer. We would call him a "religious" person in the best sense of the word. He seems not to have been a Jewish proselyte, and he knew nothing of the Old Testament, but he believed in God and had taught his household to do likewise.

Perhaps the first great truth that emerges from the conversion of Cornelius is that "religion" and morality are simply not adequate. They do not meet God's requirements. They do not "justify" a person or make him "righteous" in God's sight.

Cornelius, for all his goodness and his religion, was not saved (cf. 11:14).

Many persons resemble this man. They are faithful in the discharge of their religious practices.

They would be shocked if you told them that because they had never put their trust in Christ they are lost. They differ from Cornelius in one important detail. When God spoke to this Roman, he was sensitive to his spiritual lack and gladly sent to Peter for help.

Violating Custom

It was highly unconventional for Peter to have any unnecessary contacts with Gentiles. When the apostle invited Cornelius' messengers into Simon's house for the night (v. 23), he was violating Jewish custom. But Peter had learned, from his vision of the sheet, that the ceremonial distinctions of Judaism had served their purpose and were now to be discarded. He was learning that God's program is fluid—that the Lord is not limited to the traditions, customs, or prejudices of men. God is sovereign. He is free to modify His ways of working. He is not obliged to observe the fences and barricades, the forms and symbols of "religion," within which men sometimes try to limit Him. Where obstructions to His grace exist, God is free to destroy them. He is irresistible and omnipotent.

God was finished with the provisions of the Mosaic law that had long separated Jew from Gentile. The "barrier of the dividing wall" (Eph. 2:14) was beginning to come down. The glad tidings of salvation were to go freely to the ends of the earth, to all men everywhere.

To explain his presence at the home of a Gentile, Peter told Cornelius, "God has shown me that I should not call *any* man unholy or unclean."

Of course the distinction between Jew and Gentile is only one of the many barriers that divide people and tend to keep men from Christ.

How would your church, or your Sunday School class, react if a black Christian couple were to apply for membership? How would members feel about receiving an ex-convict or a family on welfare? Probably they would not forbid their attending your church, but would such folks really be assimilated into the fellowship of your congregation?

And how about folks with little education, or who do manual labor? How about Puerto Ricans, Chicanos, or lower-class Italians or Poles? How about unattractive people or those with no talents? And what of young men with long hair?

God's people today need desperately to show the world that the love of God goes out to *all* men, including neglected minorities, the unwanted, and those who have failed to "make it." This is not a doctrinal abstraction. It is a *fact*.

And if "undesirables" don't feel the love of God reaching them through us, how *are* they going to become aware of it?

Talk Is Cheap

Hearing someone talk about God's love—on TV, at a meeting, or in a church service—means nothing at all if the people whom these needy souls know as "Christians" show them only indifference, aversion, or even hostility.

We can't take every person we meet, or even every new member of our church, into the circle of our more intimate personal friendships. One just cannot spread himself that thin. But when we are at church gatherings, we can and must reach out to, accept, and love *everyone*. Nothing does more harm to the outreach of a church than the selfish members who spend all their time with their own particular cronies at every church social, and who talk only to their own friends after the regular services.

God is love, and *we represent Him.* He lives in us. We are partakers of His nature. And "God is not one to show partiality" (v. 34). His people are not to show it, either.

The partiality with which Peter was primarily concerned made a distinction between Jew and Gentile, the two camps into which the Jews divided mankind.

Acts 10 deals with another common problem. Christians pose the hypothetical question, "Suppose a heathen, who is off the beaten track of missionaries and has never heard the Gospel, wants to be saved? Will such a man be lost because missionaries never reached him with the truth?"

Cornelius is a scriptural example of such a person. He feared God, did what he knew was right, and prayed faithfully. It seems fair to assume that he was asking God for the knowledge he needed in order to please God. He lived up to the light he had—and God gave him more light.

More than one foreign missionary has told of being approached by devout savages, hungry for the truth about God, who have traveled many miles. They have been driven by some inner compulsion, which they could not explain, which led them to set out in search of someone who could tell them the Good News that would meet the craving of their hearts.

It is safe to say that any man, anywhere in the world, who sincerely wants to be right with God, and who is willing to accept such rightness on

God's terms, may be saved. God has ways, about which we know nothing, of getting His truth to such people.

This is not to say, however, that a man can come to God through any way other than faith in Christ. He is the *only* Way, and our responsibility is to make Him known wherever men live. Beginning with the family next door.

"The man who fears Him and does what is right is welcome to Him" (10:35), Peter told Cornelius and his friends. This statement is not a description of the plan of salvation. It simply means that a man who lives by the light he has is well prepared to come to God through faith in Christ. He is a prime candidate for salvation.

Peter went on to make the plan of salvation clear to Cornelius: Jesus was crucified, but God raised Him from death and ordered His followers to proclaim Him as Judge (v. 42) and Saviour. "Through His name everyone who believes in Him has received forgiveness of sins" (v. 43).

Prepared Hearts

The hearts of Cornelius and of the friends he had thoughtfully invited to attend this session with the apostle from Joppa were prepared hearts. They were wide open to the truth. While Peter was still talking, the Holy Spirit came on them and they began speaking in tongues. Some think the gift of tongues was given this group because the occasion was the first "official" preaching of the Gospel to Gentiles, and this is called a "Gentile Pentecost."

Peter came in for questioning when he returned to Jerusalem after staying on a few days in Caesarea (10:48) to further instruct his new converts.

"You went to uncircumcised men and ate with them," the brethren accused (Acts 11:3). Perhaps they had forgotten how the Lord Jesus ate with tax collectors and sinners.

Peter refrained from replying sharply. With the calmness of a man who knows he is right, he gave a factual record (11:11-15) of his experiences in Joppa and Caesarea. Peter was not the last servant of God who has had to account for his actions to critics who, though their intentions are undoubtedly sincere, have an inadequate conception of the broadness of God's love.

After the brethren had heard Peter, "they quieted down and glorified God, saying, 'Well, then, God has granted to the Gentiles also the repentance that leads to life'" (v. 18).

This verse marks a turning point in the history of the Christian Church. For all their preconceived notions and prejudices, the Jerusalem leaders were open to God's truth. When they learned how God had opened the door of salvation to the Gentiles, they rejoiced. Their opposition to what Peter had done evaporated. They realized that God's work was bigger than their own opinions, and willingly set aside their personal prejudices.

But Peter was not the only Christian who had come to realize that it was time for a more general preaching of the Gospel. Nudged by the Holy Spirit, believers from Cyprus and Cyrene had begun preaching to Greeks (Gentiles) at Antioch and had won many converts there (vv. 20, 21). It has been suggested that because Antioch was a commercial city where various cultures met, "men naturally got their rough corners rubbed off, and religious differences that loomed so large in Judea began to look far less important" (Bruce).

The apostles at Jerusalem sent Barnabas to Antioch to check what was going on there. Barnabas was delighted at how both Jews and Gentiles were being saved. There was nothing exclusive about Barnabas. He would have been as happy to hear that a family on the wrong side of the tracks had come to Christ as to learn about the salvation of one of the town's "first" families.

Barnabas wouldn't have been annoyed even if the church at Antioch were receiving more members, just then, than the church in Jerusalem. He seems to have lacked entirely that feeling of rivalry so common among some Christians.

Barnabas also knew what some modern Christians have not learned—that new converts need *instruction.* Evangelism without indoctrination makes for superficial Christians. So Barnabas went to Tarsus, where Saul had been living for several years, and brought the latter back to Antioch. Then for a whole year the two of them met with the believers there and "taught a large crowd" (v. 26, PH).

It was at Antioch that believers were for the first time called "Christians" (v. 26), which means "Christ's people."

11
Midnight
Jail Delivery
Acts 12

When someone mentions "the power of God," what do you think of? Does this expression bring to your mind thoughts of earthquakes, tornadoes, or hurricanes? Do you link God's power to natural disasters of one kind or another?

Many people do.

Insurance companies, as you know, refer to such unpredictable and unpreventable calamities as "acts of God." They certainly give the impression, in doing so, that God is on the side of destruction and trouble!

We often associate the concept of *power* with the physical or political areas of life. The word makes us think of a huge dynamo, a diesel engine, a space rocket, or a dictator. These are all symbols of power.

But God's power is by no means limited to the physical or political realms. It is effective in *every* area of life. And in Acts 12 we learn about two men who encountered it head-on.

Peter was one of these men. God's power delivered him from prison and saved his life.

King Herod Agrippa was the other. God's power struck him down in his prime.

Out of Prison

Herod the king, usually called Agrippa, was a grandson of Herod the Great, who ruled in Jerusalem when Christ was born. Agrippa, who reigned from A.D. 41-44, was a student of Judaism and was always happy to please the Jewish religious leaders if doing so didn't inconvenience him. He has the dubious distinction of being the first political (rather than religious) leader to persecute the Christians.

Herod's first action against the Church was to execute James, the brother of John, who had been one of the three apostles closest to Jesus. When he saw how happy this made the Jews, Herod arrested Peter. He put him in prison until after the Passover, for the Jews would have been offended if even a Christian had been put to death during the high holy days. Jesus called such inconsistency "straining out a gnat and swallowing a camel" (cf. Matt. 23:24). It is hypocrisy of the worst sort.

Herod may have remembered how Peter had previously (5:19) escaped from jail. This time he took no chances. He assigned 16 soldiers, working in squads of four, to watch over Peter. The apostle was chained between two soldiers, with two more at the door of his cell. In addition, the regular prison keepers were on duty.

One of the wonderful "buts" of the Bible occurs in verse 5: "So Peter, was being kept in prison, but from the church prayer on his behalf was unceasingly made to God" (BERK).

In prayer sessions at the famous Keswick Bible

Conference in England, it is requested that people pray briefly and to the point. Have you ever, at a prayer meeting, heard public prayer that has rambled on and on, dealing only in generalities and never really asking God for anything in particular? Many believe that the prayers of the Christians for Peter must have been specific. They were asking God for the apostle's release. They may not even have said, ". . . if it be Thy will." They may have waited on God until they felt they *knew* His will, and then prayed accordingly.

But how can prayer get a man out of prison? Many people think it is as impossible to pray someone out of jail as for a child to stop an express train by saying "Whoa!"

But prayer is power. Earnest, believing prayer lays hold on the omnipotence of God—and then things happen.

We should never say, because we cannot give advice or material relief, that we cannot help a person whose need is great. *We can pray,* and there is no way of measuring the power of the prayers we offer for those who are sick, in danger, or serving the Lord as pastors, missionaries, evangelists, or otherwise.

And if we intercede faithfully, we should not be surprised if God enables us to be of "practical" help in making some of our prayers come true.

On the very night before Herod was to bring Peter out for trial and probable execution, God's angel awoke Peter and told him to get dressed quickly. The fact that Peter faced death the next day had not afflicted him with insomnia. Most of us probably would not have had to be awakened, even if we'd taken a tranquilizer.

Some people say, because the Greek word for

"angel" also means "messenger," that the visitor to Peter's cell was not an angel but some human being acting as God's messenger. This sounds logical, but it doesn't explain how this "messenger" got into the prison and into Peter's cell, how Peter's chains fell off, how the guards "happened" to be in a supernaturally induced slumber, or how Peter and the "messenger" got out through the locked doors and past the keepers. "Explanations" of Scripture miracles often leave a lot to be explained!

Only when the angel had walked a block down the street with him did Peter realize that he was not dreaming—that he had been delivered from prison by the power of God.

It is dangerous to "spiritualize" Scripture narratives, for what one reads into them is often limited only by one's imagination. Surely, however, this miraculous deliverance of Peter illustrates how God can and often does deliver His people from the chains of adverse circumstances.

Our adverse circumstances may be something relatively trivial—being lost in the country on a late-evening car trip. It may be something of considerable importance, such as facing major surgery. It may be the need for constant effort in getting along with a cantankerous neighbor or a difficult boss. It may be bondage to a sinful habit that spoils our testimony and robs us of assurance. Whatever it may be, God is able to give us victory over it.

Perhaps you are asking, at this point, "How about James? Didn't the Church pray for him? If not, why not? If so, why wasn't *he* saved, too? Isn't God impartial?"

These are honest questions, and there is no answer for them that will satisfy some of the people who ask them.

Undoubtedly the Church prayed for James, but God saw that James' work had been completed and that there was more work left for Peter to do. So the Lord allowed the enemies of the Church to put James to death so that he might go home to glory, but led the Church to pray with confidence for Peter. Then God saw to it that Peter's life was spared.

God does not allow things to happen without good reasons. When we encounter bitter disappointments, when the person most important to us is removed at what appears to be exactly the wrong time, we must remember that God loves His people more than they love themselves. No matter how dark the present may be, He never deserts them. And when we cannot understand His "failure" to answer our prayers, we can and must accept what He allows to come to us as His good, acceptable, and perfect will.

"But," some may ask, "if it was God's will to deliver Peter, would He not have done so even if the Church had not prayed?"

Perhaps so. But, on the other hand, in many cases it may be God's will to do something for His people *if they ask Him to*. Failure to pray may deprive us of much that God is ready to give us in response to our petitions. "You do not have because you do not ask" (James 4:2).

When Peter realized what had happened, he made at once for the home of Mary, mother of John Mark, where he knew he would find some of the believers. He probably arrived there in the small hours of the morning. He knocked on the outer door.

A young woman named Rhoda came to answer

his knock, but when she recognized Peter's voice she dashed back to tell the group—without ever unlocking the door for Peter.

"You are crazy!" (wms), they told her. When she "insisted up and down that it was so" (berk), they decided that Peter's angel was at the door.

A church in the farm belt decided, after a prolonged drought, to hold a meeting to pray for rain. A little girl showed up at the meeting with an umbrella, but no adults came so prepared to see their prayers answered.

Many Christians seldom take God's prayer promises literally, to their own loss. When their prayers are answered, they are sometimes actually *surprised*.

God answered the prayers of Peter's friends in spite of their seeming lack of faith.

Once they had let Peter in, he "shushed" them and told them, quietly and quickly, just what had happened. He asked them to report his escape to James, the Lord's brother (who later presided over the Jerusalem Council, Acts 15, and seems to have been a leader in the Church).

Then Peter "departed and went to another place" (v. 17). There is no reason to believe that he went to Rome to establish a church there. More likely he "went underground" for the time being. We next meet him at the Jerusalem Council, some six years later (15:7).

Peter has a prominent place in the first 12 chapters of The Acts, but he is not even mentioned in the last 13 chapters.

Fatal Attack

The second man in this chapter to encounter

the power of God was King Herod, who had imprisoned Peter and who, in spite of his pro-Jewish inclinations, was extremely profligate and immoral.

Annoyed when the prison keeper could not produce his prize prisoner, Herod ordered that the guards who had been in charge of the apostle be put to death. Then he took off for a vacation at Caesarea.

The king was "very angry" (v. 20) with the people of Tyre and Sidon, but because these cities enjoyed friendly relations with Rome he dared not attack them with military force. It is thought he had to be satisfied with imposing trade restrictions on them, and that they had bribed Blastus, his chamberlain (v. 20), to negotiate a settlement of their differences.

On the appointed day Herod put on his "best suit," a gown made entirely of silver plates, and made a speech to these subjects. They applauded wildly. They "kept crying out, 'The voice of a God, and not of a man!'" (v. 22)

Had you been Herod, what would *you* have done?

What *do* you do when someone gives you credit you don't deserve?

King Herod probably would never have claimed to be a god, but he didn't deny the pleasant allegation that he was one. He simply said nothing, and probably felt quite smug about the impression he was creating. It doesn't seem to have occurred to him that the compliment was spoken with tongue in cheek, and that his subjects were buttering him up to get a favor from him.

"And immediately an angel of the Lord struck him" (v. 23). Not because he had executed James. Not because he had put Peter in prison. This judgment fell because "he did not give God the glory" (v. 23).

Flattery has been the downfall of many a man. It isn't always easy to set people straight at the expense of your own vanity, but Paul and Barnabas, when they were later faced by this same temptation, followed the course of modesty and truthfulness, with happier results (14:11-15).

Luke's account of Herod's unusual death is substantially the same as that reported by Josephus, the secular Jewish historian, who says the king suffered agonizing pain for five days before he expired. Josephus neglects one "small detail" that Luke mentions—that the king's death was the result of God's judgment.

And so God gave His Church victory in her first brush with the secular authorities.

No wonder "the word of the Lord continued to grow and to be multiplied" (v. 24).

Such is the record of the encounter of two men with the power of God. As we have seen, the effect of God's power on a person depends on that person's relationship to God.

If one is rightly related to God through personal trust in His Son, God's power will bless, prosper, and strengthen him.

But if one is not rightly related to God, one will some day encounter God's power in judgment and destruction.

There is no middle road.

12
Missionary
Men
Acts 13

Acts 13, recording events that took place 15 or 16 years after Pentecost, has been called the "watershed" of the entire book. Until then, Jerusalem had been the headquarters of the Church, and Peter had been the recognized leader. But from chapter 13 on, the Apostle Paul becomes the principal personality and the church at Antioch (in Syria) becomes the main center of Church activity.

And the era of foreign missions begins.

Americans spend a great deal more on pet foods than they do on missions, but missions have always been of utmost importance in the eyes of God. The remainder of The Acts emphasizes the great missionary outthrust of early Christianity, which involved Paul in spreading the Good News across the known world of that day.

The church at Antioch had been enjoying healthy growth. A prophet there, named Agabus, had predicted a famine which occurred in the reign of Emperor Claudius (A.D. 41-54). During this famine, the Antioch church sent relief funds back to Jerusalem with Barnabas and Paul (11:28-30), after which the men had returned to their ministry in Antioch (12:25).

The Antioch church was supplied with prophets and teachers (v. 1), but up to this time there was apparently no one whose special project it was to promote the outreach of the Gospel in line with the Great Commission (Matt. 28:19, 20) and Jesus' parting words (Acts 1:8). The Church didn't yet have a "missionary committee."

The Lord had used persecution to pry His people loose from the previous comfort and relative safety of Jerusalem, and they had carried the message of the risen Christ with them wherever they went. But until now there was no organized effort to reach new areas with the Word of life.

When God Speaks

➡ The Holy Spirit spoke about this to the Antioch church leaders while they were "ministering to the Lord and fasting" (v. 2). "Ministering" is from the Greek word from which we get "liturgy"—it means they were worshiping God. Because to them God was the greatest reality in life, at times they set aside eating in their preoccupation with Him. It was in such a time of worship and meditation that the Spirit revealed their new missionary assignment to them.

If Christians today were more occupied with God they would be less puzzled about discovering His will.

➡ With fasting, prayer, and the laying on of hands (v. 3), the Antioch church commissioned Barnabas and Paul as missionaries—but only after the two had been chosen by the Holy Spirit. Apart from God's calling and ordination, the ordination of men is useless. When men ordain their fellow men without regard to the Lord's will, God's work does not prosper.

The church sent Barnabas and Paul away (v. 3), but it was also the Holy Spirit who sent them out (v. 4). "Cooperation" between God and man is necessary.

The responsibility of the Antioch church toward the work to which these men were "separated" involved more than merely ordaining them and asking God's blessing on them. It no doubt included faithful prayer and financial support. It included an interest in their work that continued until they had returned and given a report (14:26, 27) to believers in the home church.

It is the duty of an individual to go when God calls, but it is the duty of a church to provide support for those who answer God's call.

Sometimes a church assumes only a small part of the support of each of a large number of missionaries. This gives the people of the church an interest in many fields of foreign service. But when a church contributes to the support of more than 50 missionaries, it is almost impossible for members to get personally acquainted with more than a few of them.

Some churches support only a few missionaries, but support them substantially, perhaps even fully. When the missionary comes home, such churches sometimes provide a furlough home for him, and he is able to rest and refresh himself because he doesn't need to do deputation work among a dozen or more other churches that contribute to his support.

On the Apostle Paul's first missionary journey

he and Barnabas took young John Mark (v. 5) with them as a helper. We might call him a missionary intern. He was a nephew of Barnabas and the son of a well-to-do Christian woman in Jerusalem in whose home the Christians were accustomed to meet (cf. 12:12).

For some unexplained reason, Mark soon left Paul and his uncle and returned home (13:13). It may be that he was afraid of a journey into the interior, or that he couldn't get along with Paul, or that he was homesick. His was not the last case of inability to adjust to missionary life. Before mission boards gave candidates the specialized tests and training most of them now receive, inability to adjust was responsible for many failures on the field.

How Does God Speak?

The Bible doesn't tell us precisely *how* the Holy Spirit communicated with men in the Early Church. Sometimes He used a vision (as in 16:9), but on other occasions it seems that perhaps a strong sense of "oughtness" (or "ought-not-ness") may have served the purpose. When a person is filled with the Spirit (a condition which should be true of every Christian) He is sensitive to the leading of God. When such a person reaches a prayerful conviction, he may act on it confidently, for he has "the mind of Christ" (1 Cor. 2:16).

It is not likely that Paul and Barnabas set out on a preplanned itinerary. On Paul's second journey, God gave him on-the-spot leading (16:6, 7, 9), and such guidance may have been given on his first journey, too.

The missionary trio went first to the island of

Cyprus, where Barnabas had once lived. It's not a bad idea to begin your work for the Lord right at home—though usually that isn't the *easiest* place to start.

The proconsul of Cyprus, a man named Sergius Paulus, was a person of keen intelligence. He was interested in the Gospel and wanted to hear more about it. As you would expect, Satan offered opposition, in the person of the proconsul's court magician. This gentleman was probably afraid his job would go down the drain if Sergius became a Christian, and he did his best to frustrate the apostles, contradicting and cursing them.

Usually, "the servant of the Lord must . . . be gentle unto all men" (2 Tim. 2:24, 25, av). When a person is keeping someone else from believing the Gospel, however, stronger treatment may be needed. Paul, filled with the Holy Spirit (v. 9), announced that the magician would be temporarily blinded, and soon after this happened the proconsul believed on Christ. There's no substitute for Holy Spirit power in overcoming obstacles to God's work.

Few Details Now

From this point on, Morgan points out, the narrative becomes more and more selective. Luke records only occasional incidents and gives few details, in order to outline for us the method the Spirit used in carrying on His work. It is important, as you read The Acts, that you focus on "the big picture."

After John Mark left them at Perga, in Pamphylia, Paul and Barnabas came to Antioch in Pisidia (vv. 13, 14). There they went to the synagogue on Saturday to worship with their fellow Jews. As was customary, the synagogue "ruler" invited guests to say a few words (cf. v. 15).

Paul's sermon was addressed to Jews, proselytes, and Gentiles friendly to the Jewish religion. He showed how God had been at work in His dealings with Israel (vv. 16-25), and his introduction would have appealed strongly to his hearers.

Paul knew that if we are to attract men to the Gospel, we must "speak their language." We must use words they can understand and concepts they are familiar with. *What* we say, as Christians, is unchanging, but we must express the message in the words and thought-patterns of current life.

In the second part of his message (vv. 26-37), Paul "preached Christ," quoting Old Testament Scripture to demonstrate that our Lord was the fulfillment of the prophetic message. The Resurrection was prominent in the sermon, and by it Paul proved that the Lord Jesus fulfilled God's promises to His people. He is the Son of God, the hope of Israel, and the Saviour of the world.

God offers men much more, in Christ, than forgiveness. He offers them justification (v. 39), which is "an act of God, on the basis of His Son's death, declaring a believing sinner *righteous*" (Newell). A justified person is the same, in relation to God, as if he had never sinned.

The only requirement for such justification is faith. When any person trusts Christ as His Saviour, no record of sin is left against him. Christians are not paroled criminals—they are people who have been restored to full favor with God.

Paul's sermon was frankly evangelistic. He was talking to unsaved persons. This message is definitely not a model for the Sunday morning congregational worship in the typical evangelical church.

After the service, Paul and Barnabas answered questions, did "personal work," and promised another sermon the next weekend.

Turning Point

When "the whole city" (v. 44) turned out the following Saturday, the Jews grew jealous because *they* didn't attract such crowds. They began cursing and contradicting Paul, and this led to an action that became a pattern for the apostles' subsequent ministry:

"Since you repudiate it [God's message]," he told them, "and judge yourselves unworthy of eternal life, we are turning to the Gentiles" (v. 46).

Paul never ceased to consider himself in debt to the Jews as well as to the Gentiles (Rom. 1:14), and his interest in his own people never waned (9:1-3), but he now began to exercise that ministry which was to gain him the title, "apostle of the Gentiles" (Rom. 11:13).

The Gentiles rejoiced, of course (v. 48), but the Jews of the city instigated a movement that caused Paul and Barnabas to have to leave town. The Jews could not accept the truth that they had no monopoly on the grace of God and that His love extends outside the limits of Abraham's children.

Jesus had told His men, "Whenever they persecute you in this city, flee to the next" (Matt. 10:23), and this is just what Paul and Barnabas did. They shook the dust of Pisidian Antioch from their feet and went on to Iconium, rejoicing and filled with the Holy Spirit (v. 52).

The Spirit, who called Paul and Barnabas into the first missionary venture of the Early Church, is still calling men and women into God's service today. Keep your ears open for His voice! He may want you to be a farmer, a businessman, a professional man, a housewife, or a nurse—but don't rule out the possibility of His calling you, even at a "late" time in life, to be a teacher, a pastor, or a missionary. And as Spurgeon put it, "If God has called you to be a missionary, forbid that you should shrivel up into being a king!"

If God doesn't want you to go to the foreign field, do what you can to send others. Give! Pray! Write letters! Send tapes! Take a genuine interest in the field. And keep in mind that God wants to use you right in your own community.

The Sunday School accounts for 85 percent of new church members and 95 percent of our pastors and missionaries. What are you doing about this tremendous field of service? Should you be teaching? Encouraging those who are teaching?

Christian leaders have coined the challenging slogan, "The world for Christ in this generation." If this great objective is to be achieved, all of us will have to work a lot harder than we've been working. The world is the field, and the field, at home and abroad, is white unto the harvest.

Your responsibility is to pray that the Lord of the harvest will send out laborers (Matt. 9:38).

And having prayed, perhaps you will be aware that part of the answer to your prayer is for God to send *you*.

13
Missionary Methods

Acts 14

Someone asked William Turner, the distinguished British painter of the Nineteenth Century, the secret of his success.

"I have no secret," said Turner, "but hard work."

Many a man or woman who "has arrived" will testify that achievement is one part inspiration and nine parts perspiration. Such individuals have risen to the top by virtue of their willingness to keep everlastingly at it. "They, while their companions slept, were toiling upward through the night" (Longfellow). Clock-watchers, whose chief interests are their coffee breaks and their vacations, seldom achieve distinction.

In Christian service, too, persistence and hard work are of great importance. The records found in The Acts, though they are fragmentary, leave no doubt in our minds about how energetically the early disciples worked at telling people about Jesus Christ. Paul and Barnabas, on their missionary journey, are striking examples of vigorous performance. We do well to imitate them.

This missionary journey, recorded in Acts 13 and 14, is a model from which we learn a good deal about the conduct of such a project in the Early Church. Many of these principles apply to God's work in our world today.

We saw, in Acts 13, that missionary work is to be undertaken as the Holy Spirit directs, that missionary personnel are to be chosen by the Spirit and ordained and supported by the Church, and that the missionary message centers in Christ. We saw, too, that we may expect Satan to oppose vigorously any attempt to spread the Gospel.

Acts 13:46 marks Paul's definite decision to tell the Gentiles about the grace of God, but he never stopped going "to the Jew first" when he came to a new town. When he and Barnabas arrived at Iconium (14:1), for example, they went at once to the local synagogue. It was customary for the synagogue ruler to invite visiting rabbis and teachers to be guest speakers. This practice provided Paul with a ready-made audience, for the Jews regularly gathered each Saturday, or Sabbath, in their synagogues.

Paul's sermon at Iconium isn't recorded, but he "spoke in such a manner that a great multitude believed, both of Jews and of Greeks" (v. 1). The Greeks (Gentiles) in view were probably proselytes to Judaism or those who were at least interested in becoming proselytes.

Satan Will Fight

Maybe "nothing suceeds like success," but it is also true that in God's work nothing stirs up the devil like success. Opposition to the truth was not long in showing itself in Iconium (v. 2).

The unbelieving Jews poisoned the minds of the Gentiles, and both factions became angry against Paul.

The Jews, as we have already seen, usually headed resistance to the Gospel (13:45, 50). They were the chief opponents of the apostle in Iconium (14:2) and also made trouble for him in Lystra and Derbe (v. 19).

That Paul was giving them first opportunity to hear and receive the Gospel meant nothing to the Jews. They were well satisfied with their own religion, thank you, and could do nicely without the Good News.

"Isn't it a fact," they would demand, in effect, "that truth is unchanging? Is Jehovah any different today than He was in the days of Abraham? We want no truck with religious innovation!"

It is of course true that God and His truth are unchanging, but God often uses new vehicles to carry His truth, and new approaches to convince men of it. We have learned a great deal, in recent years, about the science of communication. Christians need not be reluctant to use the fruits of this knowledge in communicating the Gospel.

(Incidentally, whether a method is effective or not does not depend on how "scientific" it is, or on its having been recommended by some "expert," but on the extent to which the Holy Spirit uses it to make sinful men into "new creations.")

We need to remind people constantly that being a Christian is much more than accepting a certain creed. It is having a life-giving relationship with God through personal faith in Jesus Christ.

The apostles continued their work in Iconium in spite of the opposition (v. 3), relying on the Lord for protection. And the Lord, on His part, gave them ability to perform "signs and wonders" —probably miracles of healing—to authenticate their message.

A salesman may divide a list of prospects into those he thinks are possible customers and those he regards as unlikely. He does not expect to sell his product to *all* of them. Paul's preaching of the Gospel divided Iconium (v. 4), and some of the poor "prospects" became quite menacing. When the opposition got really dangerous, Paul and Barnabas left (vv. 5, 6). They weren't unwilling to die for their faith, but they knew God had more work for them to do elsewhere and that it was important for them to go on living.

Paul was persistent. It was impossible to discourage or intimidate him. When he was thrown out of one city, he went on to another, and wherever he went he carried the Good News.

How do we react if the person to whom we are witnessing insults us or slams the door in our face? Does it discourage us for weeks or months?

Actually, few people to whom we talk about the Lord are going to insult us. A vast majority will receive us kindly and treat us courteously. They may not agree with us, but we will not get the manhandling that Paul so frequently got in those days when folks were much less subtle.

It is interesting to note that Paul usually preached in settled communities. They are called "cities" in the New Testament. Some, such as Rome (population, one million), Corinth (250,000), and Ephesus (225,000), were great cities, but many of the others were not much more than small towns, though they were the population centers of that day. Paul seems to have worked toward getting churches started in these "urban" areas.

Need Other Christians

Christians thrive best when they are with other Christians. They develop better spiritually when they can worship, study, and pray together, and when they can serve and help one another as members of Christ's body. Someone has even said, "You can't be a Christian alone." Though this is hardly to be taken literally, it is undeniable that believers need fellowship in the corporate group which is the body of Christ.

This is one reason why Paul launched new churches in the towns. The assemblies would thrive there, not only because there were more people to draw on but because believers could minister to one another more readily. And with a thriving church in the town, the message would spread out to individuals in the surrounding countryside.

At Lystra and Derbe, which were in Lycaonia ("wolf-land"), Paul found himself speaking to people of the crudest kind, uncultured and probably quite uncouth. Such people, though, have the same heart-hunger and spiritual need as the sophisticated aristocrats of modern suburbia—needs which only the Gospel can meet completely.

A young Chinese student visiting in an American home was asked, "What is the chief difference between your people and those of the United States."

"The slant of the eyebrows," he replied.

Regardless of minor differences, all men are sinners and need salvation. The message is the same for all, but our manner of telling it will vary according to the individuals we hope to reach.

Paul and Barnabas unintentionally got off to a wonderful start at Lystra by healing a cripple. This caused the natives to believe that Barnabas was Jupiter (or Zeus), father of the gods, and that Paul was Mercury (or Hermes).

King Herod had accepted this sort of flattering treatment (12:23) with a good deal of short-lived pleasure. It is always a nice feeling to have folks think better of us than we deserve. But Paul and Barnabas had better sense. When they saw preparations being made to offer a sacrifice to them (v. 13), they stopped the proceedings, though only with great difficulty.

Paul's remarks on this occasion hardly constitute a sermon. His objective was to show the people that he and Barnabas were human beings, not gods. Beyond that, he wanted to turn them from the worship of idols ("these vain things") to belief in "a living God, who made the heaven and the earth and the sea, and all that is in them" (v. 15).

Keeping in mind that he was dealing with Gentiles who did not have the Scriptures, Paul told his hearers that Jehovah God is the Source of everything good, including rain, the fruitfulness of the fields, man's food, and the joy of life (v. 15). He urged his listeners to worship God, not their idols.

Paul's work in Lycaonia was cut short by the arrival of Jews from Iconium. These determined troublemakers won over the men who were so recently bent on worshiping the apostle, and together they stoned him and dragged him out of town as dead. Human favor is often short-lived, and today's hero may be forgotten tomorrow.

Many believe that the stoning killed Paul, and that God raised him from the dead. Even if that is not the case, his instantaneous recovery was a great miracle—no hospitalization, no medication, no period of recuperation. He simply got to his feet in the presence of his anxious friends, brushed the dust off his clothes, and returned into the city! The very next day, he went on to Derbe. God's servant is immortal until his work has been finished.

The remainder of the chapter is of extreme importance for the insight it gives us into Paul's missionary methods.

More Than Evangelism

Paul and Barnabas returned to Lystra, Iconium, and Antioch, "strengthening the souls of the disciples, encouraging them to continue in the faith, and saying, 'Through many tribulations we must enter the kingdom of God'" (v. 22).

These missionaries realized that their work was not complete when they had won a group of converts and established a local church in a city. They knew that new Christians, like newborn babies, need special nurture and loving attention.

They strengthened their new converts with a series of Bible studies. Don't picture a group of believers seated in a living room, each one with a black leather Bible in his lap. There were no Bibles. Paul and Barnabas didn't carry with them the hand-lettered scrolls from which the Scripture was read at synagogue services. They had memorized whole portions of the Old Testament, and would quote from their retentive minds, commenting on, interpreting, and applying God's Word.

Paul encouraged his converts to continue in the faith (v. 22). Whether we talk about the perseverance of the saints or the preservation of the saints, it is those who continue to the end who will be rewarded. New Christians face many temptations to drop out. They may lose their old friends or their jobs, or their families may turn against them. Sometimes they are not quickly accepted into the Christian community. They need *lots* of encouragement.

Paul reminded the new believers that "many tribulations" line the road to the kingdom. We make a mistake if we tell people the pathway to heaven is bordered by sweet flowers and shady trees.

It is touching to read that Paul commended his new converts to the Lord (v. 23). That is, he prayed for those who had come to Christ under his teaching. Continuing intercessory prayer had a large part in his follow-up ministry, and we dare not neglect it in ours. New Christians need Bible study, personal encouragement, and much earnest intercession.

Paul and Barnabas revisited the churches they had started in Perga and Attalia. Then they returned to Antioch after having been absent for about two years. They reported to the church there how the Lord had used them, and especially how Gentiles were coming to faith in Christ. They continued "a long time" (v. 28)—perhaps about three years—in Antioch with the disciples.

14
No Legalism, but—

Acts 15

Is it right for a Christian to engage in the following practices?

Dancing   Mixed bathing
Television watching   Movie-going
Card playing   Reading novels

Some Christians, sincerely eager to live holy lives, roundly condemn most of these activities. Others, equally sincere, engage in most of these practices with clear consciences.

There are two extremes to which you can go in this regard, and both are wrong.

• The first extreme is the notion that because you are saved by grace, no rules or regulations limit your conduct. Those who hold this position, sometimes called "only-believism," like to remind us that Christians are "free from the Law" and that a person who has been born again has liberty to do as he pleases.

Actually, Christians *are* free from the Law— they need not obey it to earn salvation. Eternal life is God's gift; we can neither earn it nor keep it by obeying the Law or any other rules.

But God expects His children to obey Him—not so that they may be saved but *because they have been saved.* Love and gratitude, not an effort to win God's acceptance, are to motivate them. And a Christian may do as he wants only insofar as he is led by the Holy Spirit, in which case the Spirit will unfailingly cause him to want to do what God wills.

• The other of the two extremes is legalism. Some earnest Christians lack an adequate conception of the completeness of Christ's sacrifice. They feel that though they have been saved by faith, they are made more spiritual by living according to certain rules which are often man-made. They sometimes depend largely on negatives. By not engaging in certain practices they feel they are living "separated" lives. That *can* be legalism.

Early Church Legalism

The Early Church faced the problem of legalism. It was the issue behind Paul's writing Galatians, in which he condemns this attitude in no uncertain terms. And it was the issue that confronted the church at Antioch in A.D. 50 or thereabouts.

For nine or ten years the Church had been admitting Gentile converts to membership on their profession of faith in Christ. Now, however, "some men came down from Judea and began teaching the brethren [at Antioch], 'Unless you are circumcised according to the custom of Moses, you cannot be saved'" (v. 1). Paul calls these men "false brethren" (Gal. 2:4). They were not believers and they had no authorization from the Jerusalem church (Acts 15:24). Their legalistic and unorthodox views "unsettled" (wms) the new Christians.

The upshot was that the Antioch church had a great discussion of the subject, with much debate, and finally sent a delegation, including Paul and Barnabas, to Jerusalem. They did not go to get a ruling from "Holy Mother Church," but so that those involved might meet face to face, talk out their differences, and look for the leading of the Holy Spirit in the dispute.

At Jerusalem, the Antioch delegation found that some Pharisees who had been converted to Christianity agreed with the legalistic teachers (v. 5). These Pharisees were *not* "false brethren," but they were certainly mistaken. Sincere Christians *can* be wrong.

The apostles and elders met to look into the matter (v. 6). The debate was long and earnest, both sides taking part. It would appear that the legalists were plainly a minority.

The Judaizers did not question the admission of Gentiles into the Church. That question had already been settled (11:18) to their satisfaction. But they reminded the others that the Pentateuch made circumcision a condition of "salvation" (cf. Gen. 17:14). Even Abraham had been circumcised (Rom. 4:10, 11).

The zeal of the legalists for God's Word was commendable, but these people overlooked one all-important truth. The death of Christ had brought a change. The Law, "a *shadow* of the good things to come" (Heb. 10:1), had been replaced by the *reality* of God's grace. It had served its purpose.

Two Good Reasons

After giving the proponents of legalism every

opportunity to speak (it is often an advantage to speak *last*), the Apostle Peter gave the meeting two important reasons why Gentiles should not be circumcised:

• God *had visited* them and had given them the Holy Spirit (Acts 15:7, 8). Peter was referring, of course, to his own experience at the home of Cornelius (chap. 10), when a number of Gentiles had been saved without benefit of circumcision. This, he said, clearly indicated that Gentiles and Jews stood on the same ground before God (v. 9). Both were saved (or cleansed) by faith.

• It made no sense, said Peter, to put Gentiles under a law which even the Jewish Christians themselves could not keep (v. 10). If the Law were adequate for salvation, why was the Gospel necessary? The Hebrew believers had been saved because they had by faith entered into the grace of the Lord Jesus—and this was exactly how the Gentiles were also being saved (v. 11).

Peter established the fact, then, that Gentiles *had been* saved without being circumcised or obeying the Ten Commandments. The implication of his remarks was that circumcision and the Law, though both were ordained by God, had served their purpose and were no longer necessary.

None of the Hebrew Christians at the meeting, observed Peter (cf. v. 11), would claim that works of the Law had saved them. Why, then, should they insist on such works in Gentiles?

Conclusion Voiced

Finally James, brother of the Lord Jesus and apparently the leader of the Jerusalem church, summarized the conclusion of the gathering. Notice that *Peter* did not do this. Peter was not the "leader of the apostles." But James was no "pope" either; he simply "gathered the sense of the meeting," as the Quakers express it. He undertook to "verbalize" the opinions of those present in a way acceptable to both the majority and the minority.

James reviewed what Peter (he calls him, here, by his Hebrew name, Simeon) had said about God's interest in the Gentiles. He linked Peter's conclusion with a rather loose quotation from Amos 9:11, 12 (Acts 15:16-18). The manner in which he used this Old Testament Scripture, changing the words somewhat, need not disturb us. God does not act contrary to His Word, but He is its final interpreter. The Holy Spirit, who is Author of all Scripture, certainly is free to modify the Old Testament in quoting from it in the New Testament.

The point of this Amos quotation, says Bruce, is that the presence of believing Jews in the Church fulfilled the prediction of the restoration of David's tabernacle (v. 16). The presence of believing Gentiles fulfilled Amos' reference to "the rest of mankind" (v. 17). And since it was God's will that Gentiles come into the Church, concluded James, the Church should not put obstacles in their way (v. 19, AMP). Law-keeping and circumcision have no place in the plan of salvation. Men become children of God by putting their trust in the Lord Jesus Christ as their Saviour.

The statement that James made doubtless represented the opinion of most of those at the meeting. Nevertheless, James had more to say, suggesting that they should ask the Gentile Christians not to eat meat offered to idols, not to commit fornication, and not to eat meat from which the blood hadn't been properly drained (cf. v. 20).

These restrictions are in no sense requirements for salvation. They are included in the findings of the council in order not to ride roughshod over the more "conservative" element in the Church, or to expose weaker brothers to temptation. They express the same loving concern for other Christians that Paul later expressed in his dealing with the thorny subject of controversial practices (Rom. 14:13, 15, 21; 1 Cor. 8:13).

• The eating of meat that had been offered to idols was a vexing problem in the Early Church. The Jerusalem meeting did *not* declare that eating such meat was sinful, but suggested that Gentile Christians refrain from the practice in order not to offend Hebrew Christians to whom, on account of their background, it was repugnant.

• Nor were Gentile believers to eat meat from which the blood had not been drained. This rule was given to mankind long before the Mosaic Law, in the days of Noah (Gen. 9:4). It is not a Levitical regulation at all. Blood, even of animals, is regarded as sacred because it carries the life of the flesh and because it made atonement for the soul, or "covered" sin (Lev. 17:11).

• The third requirement, that Gentiles abstain from immorality, is not a ceremonial matter at all, but a moral one. Immorality was extremely common among Gentiles of the first century and was even part of the pagan "religious" rites of that time. Men took it pretty much for granted, as most people do today. And it was as objectionable among Jewish Christians, of course, as among Gentile believers (1 Thes. 4:3).

The reason for these three restrictions is plainly stated: "For Moses from ancient generations has in every city those who preach him, since he is read in the synagogues every Sabbath" (Acts 15: 21). The Hebrews had been taught since childhood that these practices were wrong. Why should Gentile converts offend God in the area of moral purity ("immorality") or offend their Hebrew brothers in the area of ceremonial custom?

Of One Mind

In reaching its decision, the meeting at Jerusalem was "of one mind" (v. 25). Even in difference, there can be unity. It is not necessary for every Christian in a group to have the same opinion as every other believer holds, but all God's people are to be "of one mind."

The minority, at Jerusalem, did not hold a grudge because they were overruled. The majority, on the other hand, went out of their way to keep the welfare and the feelings of the minority in view.

Sticking to this simple principle would often eliminate division in a church or other group of Christians that is harrassed by differences. All too often the majority, in a Protestant group, will ignore the rights of the minority, and the minority will secede from the majority. The way James and Peter and the others handled the dispute over legalism prevented the Church's being split into a Gentile camp and a Hebrew camp.

The apostles and the elders, "with the whole Church" (v. 22), felt it advisable to send a delegation back to Antioch with a letter (vv. 23-29) stating the conclusions that had been reached. The letter was good because it crystallized and put into permanent form the important decisions made. But the sending of a delegation was even better. There is no substitute, in cases of disagreement, for "eye-ball-to-eyeball" contact. That's probably why Jesus prescribes this treatment for the fellow Christian who sins against you (Matt. 18:15).

The letter from Jerusalem was read to the entire church at Antioch (Acts 15:30, 31), and the Gentile Christians rejoiced at their "emancipation proclamation."

And so a great and problematical issue, that might have split the Early Church wide open, was settled amicably. It was not settled, however, by taking a vote. Questions of right and wrong cannot be settled by ballot. A vote determines which side is more popular, not which side is *right*.

This thorny question was settled by a frank discussion in which both sides expressed themselves. Both parties to the dispute—the apostles and the believing Pharisees (v. 5)—were Christians. When one party is made up of unbelievers, we cannot always hope for a meeting of minds.

Both parties, also, were sincerely ready to have their differences reconciled. Both honestly believed they were right, but both were open to the evidence in the case: the testimony of Scripture and the principles on which God had obviously been working.

Most important of all, the settlement of this dispute was acceptable to both sides because it came about as the result of the work of the Holy Spirit (v. 28). The Spirit Himself, not Peter or James, was the Leader who had brought the conference to the right conclusion.

Legalism has not been confined to the first century. Its appeal has always been strong, and it has blighted every age of Church History.

Man has an inherent impulse to contribute to

his own salvation. He wants to *do* something to help get himself into heaven. He may even reject the Gospel because free salvation is "unreasonable." Some minds are so constituted that they seem to prefer bondage.

Sometimes legalism results from a sincere—but misdirected—effort to please God.

Never confuse legalism with the deep love for Christ that leads some people to give up activities they consider "worldly" so that no shadow may fall on their close walk with the Saviour. Such a holy desire may lead a Christian into a manner of life that other believers regard as "narrow" or "extreme," or even legalistic. This is not true; such Christians live as they do because they *want* to, not because they feel that they *must*.

Acts 15 shows us that Christians have freedom. It also shows us that they have obligations to others. They are not to turn their liberty into license or give offense to other believers.

Christian liberty is important, but so is Christian love.

15
Believing
in Christ

Acts 16

"Receive Christ as your Saviour."
"Believe in the Lord Jesus."
"Open your heart to the Lord."
These expressions are commonly used by Christians in telling others how they may be saved. They are three ways of saying pretty much the same thing.

But sometimes the person with whom we use these words does not really understand what we mean. In that case, his profession of faith may not be genuine because he does not realize the full significance of what he is saying.

One of these three expressions is a key verse of Acts 16. It is perhaps one of the most quoted verses of Scripture. But it is often misunderstood.

Acts 16 continues the record, begun in 15:36, of Paul's second missionary journey. Concerned for the new churches he and Barnabas had left behind them in Asia Minor, Paul proposed that they revisit them and check on their progress.

Barnabas agreed, but wanted to take John Mark, his nephew, with them. This young man had abandoned the two missionaries at Pamphylia (13:13) on their previous trip. His uncle was for giving him another chance. Paul objected strenuously, and the contention between him and Barnabas was so hot that they "split" over it. It's foolish to argue about which of the two was right, for it was probably a matter of personalities, but we know that Mark later redeemed himself in the service of Christ and that Paul found him "useful" (2 Tim. 4:11).

As a result of this disagreement, Barnabas set out for Cyprus with John Mark, and this is the last time in The Acts that he is mentioned. Paul set out with Silas (also called Silvanus), "strengthening" (Acts 15:41) the churches he and Barnabas had founded on their first trip. Churches—and individual believers—*need* more than to be given the Gospel and led to a decision. They need to be built up in the faith—to be *strengthened*. We are told that as a result of Paul's visit, the churches *were* made stronger (16:5).

We must never think, then, that we have done our complete duty by getting someone's signature on a decision card. New converts need a great deal of help if they are to become mature Christians.

Concession, Not Compromise

When Paul and Silas got to Lystra (v. 1), they took into their party a young man named Timothy. Probably Timothy had been converted on Paul's previous visit there, but he owed much of his spiritual stature to the faithful training of his mother Eunice and his grandmother Lois (2 Tim. 1:5). The entire Christian training of our children today should not be delegated to the Sunday School or to a Christian Day School. Bringing up children is a responsibility that God puts squarely on the shoulders of parents.

Timothy's mother was Jewish, but his father was a Greek and not, so far as we know, a believer. Some are surprised to read that Paul had Timothy circumcised (v. 3). Wasn't this rather inconsistent on Paul's part, in view of the decision that had just been reached in Jerusalem (chap. 15)? Some commentators have accused Paul of not practicing what he preached.

But Paul was keenly aware of the meaning of Christian liberty. He knew it makes room for a certain amount of seeming "inconsistency." He knew that God is above all "rules," even the ruling of the Jerusalem council. Some people tend to think of God as having to operate within the framework they superimpose on Him. Paul knew that having Timothy circumcised would make the young man and his message more acceptable to the Jews who knew him as an uncircumcised Gentile. Paul was sure the Lord would approve this step.

Timothy's circumcision had nothing to do with his salvation. It was simply an instance of Paul's willingness to be "all things to all men" (1 Cor. 9:19-23) so that the Gospel might not be hindered.

As Paul, Silas, and Timothy traveled across Asia Minor, they somehow had no "freedom" to preach in certain areas (Acts 16:6, 7). We aren't sure just how the Holy Spirit restricted them, but if modern Christians were more sensitive to such guidance, they would avoid much misdirected and wasted effort.

When the three missionaries got to Troas, on the shore of the Aegean Sea, their leading changed.

Here Paul had a vision at night. He saw a man of Macedonia appealing to him, saying, "Come over to Macedonia and help us" (v. 9).

The decision of the trio that God was calling them to Europe was a momentous one. It changed the whole course of Christianity. Suppose the Lord had led Paul and Silas eastward into the Orient? The history of the world would have been vastly different, for civilization as we know it has followed the Gospel, and it would undoubtedly have moved eastward with the message instead of westward to the continents of Europe and America.

The "we" here (v. 10) indicates that the writer of The Acts, Dr. Luke, had now joined the missionary party. He crossed the Aegean with Paul, Silas, and Timothy. They sailed to Neapolis and pushed on to Philippi, which soon afterward was the site of a thriving Christian church.

There must not have been 10 Jewish men in Philippi, or they would have had a synagogue. Since there was no synagogue, Paul went to the riverside to a place where people often prayed, and witnessed to the few Jewish women whom he found gathered there. Women have always played an important role in the Church. Many times they have filled the gaps left by the absence or unwillingness of men. Their experience and their judgment are valuable to the cause of Christ, and they have ministered in all sorts of ways.

The first convert to Christianity in Europe was Lydia, a business woman from Thyatira who was associated with one of the companies that produced the purple dye for which that city was famous. She seems to have been well-to-do, and since her home was large enough to accommodate the missionary party, they accepted her invitation to make their headquarters there. (Compare with Matt. 10:11.)

Before the days of Holiday Inns and Best Western Motels, hospitality was perhaps more important than it is today. Early Christians were *commanded* not to forget to entertain travelers (Heb. 13:2), and God's servants *depended* on such hospitality in their travels.

But hospitality today is also important, and there is a special blessing for the family whose home is open to the pastor and his family, missionaries on furlough, college students away from home, traveling evangelists and other visitors. To share one's home is a way of sharing oneself.

And yet there are Christians who almost never entertain. They are afraid that their home or their silverware or their dishes or their cooking may be inadequate. They fail to realize that what visitors look for in a home is not fine furniture or gourmet meals but simple, warm, sincere fellowship. Such entertaining is "more than a grace; it is a virtue."

God Did It

Paul witnessed to Lydia, but Paul did not *save* her. It was the Holy Spirit who "opened her heart to respond to the things spoken by Paul" (v. 14). It is God, and only God, who saves unbelievers. He enables them to respond, and as they do so, putting their trust in Christ, He saves them. Salvation is God's work, and only He can do it. But it is *our* responsibility to give people the message, and *theirs* to receive it. That is how sinners become children of God.

Satan opposed Paul in Philippi. A demon-possessed slave girl whose owners were cashing in on her ability to tell fortunes kept following the missionaries around, crying out, "These men are bondservants of the Most High God, who are proclaiming to you the way of salvation" (v. 17). This may sound like a good endorsement, but Paul had no wish to be endorsed by a fortuneteller, so he finally exorcised the girl's demon.

We can't be sure that this girl was saved, but what happened to her shows that the power of God is as available to a person in her lowly position as to a person who, like Lydia, is an "up-and-outer."

When the demon left the girl, she lost her ability to tell fortunes. Her owners immediately pressed charges against the missionaries, accusing them of throwing the city into confusion and proclaiming unlawful customs (vv. 20, 21). It was neither the first time (cf. Mark 5:13-17) nor the last that vested interests have opposed the spread of God's truth. When the Gospel is bad for business . . . well, men put "first things first," of course!

The chief magistrates, perhaps influenced by a large crowd that was hostile toward Paul, had him and Silas stripped, beaten with rods, and thrown into an inner dungeon. This dungeon has been discovered. It had no window or ventilator, the darkness was total, the heat oppressive, and the stench fearful. There, bleeding and sore, the two men were confined in the stocks, their legs spread apart at the most uncomfortable angle possible.

But "the legs feel no pain in the stocks when the heart is in heaven," wrote Tertullian. At midnight Paul and Silas, instead of groaning in discomfort, sang the praises of God. How the other prisoners must have wondered as they heard, coming from the inner dungeon, strains of song, perhaps some first-century equivalent to *All the*

Way My Saviour Leads Me, or *It Is Well With My Soul.*

The prisoners must have recognized God's hand when the prison walls quivered in an earthquake, for all the doors opened and their chains were unfastened—something no ordinary earthquake would do. The jailer, roused out of his sleep, was sure his prisoners had escaped. He prepared to commit suicide at once rather than face torture and execution for "negligence."

"Don't hurt yourself—we're all here!" called Paul cheerfully. The relieved man, calling for a lamp, went into the dungeon and brought the prisoners out.

"Sirs," he asked, "what must I do to be saved?"

What Did He Mean?

It is hardly likely that this pagan jailer understood the theological meaning of the word "saved," unless perhaps Paul had witnessed to him as he and Silas were being locked up for the night. More likely, the jailer wanted to know how he could save his life. But whatever he had in mind, Paul quickly directed his thoughts to the most important topic there is. Ability to turn a conversation to the way of salvation is one of the marks of a gifted personal worker.

Some current religious leaders would have advised the jailer to do his best, to help his fellow man, to develop his character, to join a church, to "get religion." Paul gave the only advice of any value: "Believe in the Lord Jesus."

But what does it *mean* to believe in Jesus?

Some people think that anyone who accepts the truth of the Gospel—who believes that Jesus Christ was God incarnate, that He died for men's sins, and that He rose again—is a Christian.

The very demons of hell know the Gospel and believe that it is true, but their knowledge and mental assent don't help them at all (James 2:19).

Knowledge of and assent to the truth are essential, but "to believe in" also means to trust oneself, or commit oneself, to Jesus Christ.

When one realizes that he is a sinner, unable to make himself acceptable to God, when he believes that Jesus Christ died for his sins on the cross and trusts Him for salvation, then one becomes a child of God, indwelt by the Holy Spirit and a partaker of the divine nature.

"Believe in the Lord Jesus, and you shall be saved, you *and your household*," the apostle said.

This does not imply, as it may seem to, that the jailer's whole family could be saved on the basis of his personal faith. No person can "believe" for someone else. Salvation was open to the jailer and to his whole household on exactly the same terms—the personal trust of each individual in Jesus Christ. *Anyone* who wants salvation and is willing to accept it on God's terms may have it and become a Christian.

Paul explained all this to the jailer and his household (v. 31), and baptized them all as they all put their trust in the Saviour. Then the jailer fed his prisoners and probably dressed their lacerated backs, rejoicing greatly that salvation had come to him and his loved ones.

At daybreak the magistrates, perhaps because Luke and Timothy had told them that Paul and Silas were Roman citizens, sent word to the jail that the prisoners were to be released at once.

Paul refused.

"They beat us publicly without any kind of trial; they threw us into prison despite the fact that we are Roman citizens. And now do they want to get rid of us in this underhand way?" he asked. "Oh, no, let them come and take us out themselves!" (v. 37, PH)

This was not the only time that Paul, as a preacher of the Gospel, demanded his rights under Roman law. God instituted the state (Rom. 13:1) and intended it for the protection of all people. We dishonor God's provision when we do not accept and use it. We find Paul, in one form or another, appealing several times for his legal rights.

The Philippian magistrates had to eat humble pie. Reluctantly, you may be sure, they came to the jail and personally released the prisoners. To have flogged a Roman citizen was a serious offense on their part, and they must have apologized profusely to their victims. The magistrates could not expel Roman citizens from the city, but they requested them to waste no time leaving (cf. v. 39).

Paul and his friends did not depart, however, without first returning to Lydia's home. They spent a little time there, encouraging the converts. It appears that they left Luke behind them to help build up the new church, and then went on their way with Timothy.

16
Talking to Intellectuals
Acts 17

A zealous personal worker had a favorite approach in witnessing.

"Where do you expect to spend eternity?" he would ask.

Sometimes people showed interest, but more often they were "turned off" and changed the subject or walked away.

All people aren't alike in their interests, and we must use our God-given judgment. We must be sensitive to the Holy Spirit's leading in how we talk to people about Christ.

Acts 17 records Paul's travels from Philippi to Thessalonica, Berea, and Athens, and tells of his experiences in these places. It includes his encounter with the Athenian philosophers, who were about as close as you could get, in that day, to modern "intellectuals."

At the Thessalonian synagogue, Paul "reasoned with them from the Scriptures" (v. 2). He always used the Word of God in his presentations. God's Word is living and energetic (Heb. 4:12, lit.) and effective. If one wants to be an effective personal worker, he must get to know the Bible. It has the answers for the questions people are asking—but one must know where in the Bible the answers are.

It was hard for the Jews to accept the fact that the Messiah had to suffer and die (Acts 17: 3). People today, too, sometimes balk at the teaching that "without shedding of blood there is no forgiveness" (Heb. 9:22). But we don't apologize for God's plan of salvation—we just state it.

The Jews in Thessalonica got a mob together—"lewd fellows of the baser sort" (AV)—to create a city-wide disturbance. The religious leaders themselves wouldn't have been guilty of rioting, but they were glad to work through the ruffians and hoodlums who were as available then as they are today.

An Upsetting Message

Paul and Silas had been quartered in the home of Jason, who was dragged before the authorities on the charge of harboring subversives. His guests, it was claimed, had been turning the world upside down (cf. v. 6).

Many people crave a message less upsetting than the Gospel. They want to be reminded that God is love and to be told that they are His children, on their way to heaven. Anyone who preaches such a "comfortable" religion will meet little trouble. But preach that forgiveness is available only on the basis of Christ's death and your message will be unpalatable to many.

Jason posted bond to assure that Paul would cause no further trouble. The disciples took the apostle by night to Berea, the next town on the

Egnatian Highway, which linked Rome with the Orient.

Even though Paul was run out of Thessalonica, he had not failed there. His two letters to the Thessalonians reveal what an active, spiritual group of Christians he left behind him.

Paul and Silas found a warm welcome in Berea. The Jews there listened gladly to the Gospel and searched the Old Testament Scriptures daily, perhaps using the scrolls kept at the local synagogue, to check the accuracy of the apostle's teaching.

The Bereans teach us the importance of knowing the Bible for ourselves. Ignorance of God's Word is inexcusable, but vast numbers of believers do not read the Bible enough, let alone study it, to be able to recognize error when they hear it.

Many of the Bereans believed, but when word of what was happening there reached Thessalonica, a delegation from that town came to Berea to harrass Paul, who therefore went on to Athens to wait for Silas and Timothy.

While waiting, Paul did some sight-seeing. Athens had a glorious history and was known even than as the cradle of democracy. It had many magnificent buildings and was a center of culture and art. The sculptures of Phidias, for instance, were famous all over the world.

Paul probably appreciated Athens, for he was an educated man, but he was distressed by the city's abandonment to idolatry. The place was full of temples, idol statues, and pagan altars. Paul was exasperated beyond endurance (v. 16, wms).

Christians and Culture

There is nothing wrong with a Christian's appreciating good art, music, and literature. God intends us to enjoy everything that is uplifting and ennobling. Even the stars, the clouds, and the sunset testify to His eternal power and Godhead (Rom. 1:20, AV), and it is not unspiritual to enjoy, or even to revel in, these good gifts provided by God.

But neither is it wrong for a Christian to be so moved by the evidences of man's depravity, and so convinced that the most important thing he can do is to acquaint sinners with the Saviour, that he will not allow himself to become preoccupied with "culture."

Paul went to a synagogue in Athens and spoke there to fellow Jews and to God-fearing Gentiles (v. 17). But he went also to the marketplace, where the Athenians spent much of their free time, and there he talked about the Lord to anyone who would listen.

The Athenians had a reputation for being intensely interested in anything that was new and different (v. 21). The same trait is much in evidence today, even among Christians. Sometimes a preacher's popularity is more enhanced by startling interpretations and bold views of prophecy than by his loyalty to the unchanging truth. It is one thing to treat old truth in fresh, vital, new ways, and quite another thing to try to produce something no one has heard of before in an effort to make a sensation.

Paul entered into discussion with the philosophers of Athens, of which there were two varieties. The Epicureans believed that the chief end of life is pleasure. Epicureus had taught that happiness is achieved by the pursuit of virtue and moral excellence, but by Paul's time his followers were teaching that the grossest kind of sensuality was part of "the good life."

The Stoics, on the other hand, pursued self-sufficiency as their goal. They had higher moral standards than the Epicureans, but were completely pagan. They believed that everything was governed by fate. Zeno, the first Stoic, committed suicide, and self-destruction was common among his followers.

Both these views of life are common today. The goal of modern followers of Epicureus is to eat, drink, and be merry. Other persons, whose views are similar to those of the Stoics, are drunk with the pride of intellect. Both are hard to reach with the Gospel.

Paul's preaching intrigued, but did not greatly impress, the philosophers. They called him a "retailer of scraps of second-hand philosophy" (v. 18, Bruce). They took him to the Areopagus, a sort of court which examined and licensed public lecturers. Four centuries earlier it had condemned Socrates.

• Paul set out to win his hearers rather than to take them by storm (cf. v. 22). "You are very religious," he told them. He did not accuse them of idolatry, but recognized their capacity for God and the fact that they yearned for something to worship.

He went on to mention that he had seen, in their city, an altar "to an unknown God" (v. 23). The Athenians were taking no chances. They had built altars to every known god and goddess, and lest they had inadvertently omitted one, they erected this additional altar to protect themselves from any oversight. No wonder Paul called them very religious!

The Unknown God

"You are correct," Paul said, in effect, "in admitting that there is One whom you do not know. Such a God *does* exist, and He is beyond the reach of your religion and your ritual. He is the very One you need to know above all others. Allow me to talk to you about Him" (cf. v. 23).

We can learn a lesson from Paul's approach. In speaking to someone about Christ, we should find some common ground, begin at some point where we can agree. We should not put a person on the defensive, at first, by pointing out his mistakes. Instead, we should look for something about which we can speak favorably—his interest in the subject, his curiosity, his belief in "God," or the fact that he has been attending church or owns a Bible.

• Realizing that a philosopher's first concern is with the origins of things, Paul first told the Athenians about God's power and sovereignty in creation (v. 24; Rom. 1:20). The universe has been produced by a supreme and intelligent Being. Any other explanation cannot be *logically* defended. Because all the evidence *demands* the existence of God, the Bible nowhere stops to argue this fact. To disbelieve in Creation is to disregard the evidence and start with the unjustifiable presupposition that, since there is no God, He could not have been the Creator!

The Creator and Lord of heaven and earth, Paul went on, obviously does not live in man-made temples (Acts 17:24). Moreover, He is the only self-existent One, and sustains everything He made. The Giver and Supporter of life, He is not in need of our human services. Our worship (ASV) adds nothing to Him. We, of course, are dependent on Him for life, breath, and everything else (v. 5).

• All mankind, Paul explained, originates from one man (v. 26). This does not mean, as some insist, that all men are children of God or spiritual brothers. They are God's offspring (v. 28) by creation, but they may *become* His children, or sons, only by receiving His Son by believing on Him (John 1:12).

Racists claim that Acts 17:26 means that God intended the black man to stay in Africa, but such misinterpretation cannot be supported. The verse simply tells us that God gave each group of human beings its own original territory (cf. Deut. 32:8). It no more teaches that the black man should have stayed in Africa than that the white man should have stayed in Europe, or the yellow man in Asia.

Paul's words were a knockout blow to Greek pride. The Athenians believed their ancestors sprang from the soil of their beloved land. They considered themselves a superior race. They heard the truth from Paul! Since all men are descended from Adam, nothing is more absurd than the contempt and pride with which some races or ethnic groups look down on others.

• God wants *all* men to be saved (1 Tim. 2:4). He wants them to "seek" Him, or "grope for Him and find Him" (Acts 17:27). Most "intellectuals" today have written off God. They no longer believe He exists or that He is a factor to be reckoned with. But there are still multitudes of people who are looking for an answer to the riddle of life. They are turning by the thousands to the occult and to false religions—even to Satan worship. The Church must reach these and all men with the Gospel.

Ours is the privilege of telling people, as Paul

told the Athenians, that God "is not far from each one of us" (v. 27). Any unbeliever who sincerely turns to God will find himself face to face with the Lord Jesus. "You will seek Me and find Me," God told men centuries ago, "when you search for Me with all your heart" (Jer. 29:13).

Quoting Athenian Poets

Paul quoted from two Greek poets. Epimenides had said, "In Him we live and move and exist," and Aretus had said, "We are His offspring" (Acts 17:28). Reason, as well as Scripture, testifies that God is man's Creator.

Paul had a sound education. He had studied hard and read widely. He was prepared to meet the Greek philosophers on their own ground.

Some of our Lord's disciples were unlearned fisherman, and God used them widely, but God does not place a premium on lack of training. Not all of us can talk intelligently to those involved in false religions or in the occult, but it is our responsibility as servants of Jesus Christ to know something about the beliefs and the thinking of the people with whom we deal, so that our witness may be more effective. That is why it is not always wise for us to shut ourselves up to Christian books and magazines for fear our minds may become polluted.

• "Since," Paul went on, "you yourselves admit that we are God's offspring, isn't it rather foolish to think that God, our Maker, is *less than* we are, or that He is represented by something fashioned by human hands?" (cf. v. 29).

God, the apostle concluded, had been patient with man's foolishness and sin (v. 30), but a new day was dawning. God commanded that all men repent because a time of judgment was coming. The Man whom God had appointed Judge was accredited by His resurrection from the dead (v. 31).

The Greeks believed in the immortality of the soul, but they could not stomach the idea of the resurrection of the body. To them, this notion "was as absurd as it was undesirable" (Bruce). But because they could say nothing against Paul's argument, they did what men in their position have often done since—they began to mock. And rather than cast his pearls before swine, Paul left, encouraged that some—including a member of the 12-man council—believed his message. Others wanted to hear more from him later.

"Why," asks Gaebelein, commenting on Paul's use of the word "repent" (v. 30), "didn't the apostle press home the Gospel and speak of the forgiveness of sins?"

The answer is that his hearers were not ready for more truth than he gave them. Paul realized that there are times when an all-out evangelistic message will not serve God's purpose. His sermon on Mars Hill in Athens was not unlike his message at Lystra (14:15-17). We may safely conclude that Paul followed the leading of the Holy Spirit in both cases.

Did Paul fail at Athens? Most scholars do not think so. God measures our "success" by our faithfulness (1 Cor. 4:2), not by the number of converts we make. Besides, a solid, fruitful church developed at Athens in the years that followed.

God's Word *doesn't* fail!

17
Encouraged by God
Acts 18

Paul did not stay in Athens long after his address on Mars Hill. Perhaps he wondered, as he left the city, why the Gospel was so poorly received by those so well equipped mentally. Perhaps the Holy Spirit gave him the basic thought of 1 Corinthians 1:26-29 at this time, for truly "not many wise according to the flesh" responded to his message at Athens.

The apostle went on to Corinth, 45 miles away. This city was a seaport and a great commercial center. Above all, it was an excessively wicked town. When people of the first century wanted to describe a completely immoral or perverted person, they would say, "He lives like a Corinthian." Even the so-called "religion" of Corinth centered on lust, and in the beautiful temple of Aphrodite (the goddess of love) were a thousand priestesses who were nothing but prostitutes.

In Corinth, Paul met Priscilla and Aquila, who became his loyal and valued friends and helpers (cf. Rom. 16:3, 4). They were from a family of good standing, loved the Lord, and knew the

Scriptures. They were refugees, having left Rome when Emperor Claudius ordered all non-Roman Jews out of the city. Paul probably met them in the synagogue, where each Jewish man would sit with others of his trade or profession. Because he and Aquila were both tentmakers, Paul went to live and work with them.

When Silas and Timothy joined Paul, they brought with them a love-gift from the churches of northern Greece. This freed Paul from having to earn a living and enabled him to devote all his time to preaching the Gospel (Acts 18:5). Paul stoutly defended the right of a Christian worker to a livelihood from those to whom he imparts spiritual blessing through his preaching and teaching (1 Cor. 9:7-15), but he had refused any gifts from the Corinthians lest they accuse him of commercializing his ministry. It is easy to see, from the Corinthian epistles, that conditions in the church at Corinth left much to be desired.

Paul "was reasoning in the synagogue every Sabbath and trying to persuade Jews and Greeks" (Acts 18:4).

Not Merely Subjective

Some people would have us believe that the Gospel is a purely subjective matter and that it appeals to the emotions rather than to the intellect. They give the impression that a good education makes it harder, not easier, to accept the Good News.

That is not what Paul believed. The Gospel *does* make an appeal to the emotions, but it is far from anti-intellectual. The Gospel rests on *historical facts*—on things that actually happened on this planet, including the virgin birth of Jesus, His life and teachings, His vicarious death, His bodily resurrection and ascension into heaven, and the coming of the Holy Spirit at Pentecost.

Paul not only proclaimed these truths, but he "reasoned" or "argued" them. He supported what he said by giving evidence—the prophecies of the Old Testament that had been fulfilled and the experiences Jesus' followers had had with Him during His lifetime and especially after His resurrection. Several times in The Acts we find the word "reasoned," which means to discuss logically, or to dialogue.

The Gospel is something we accept "on faith," but it is not unreasonable. It fits in perfectly with the teachings and prophecies of the Old Testament (with which multitudes of Christians are totally unfamiliar), and it meets perfectly the spiritual and emotional needs of men of all times and places.

The Jews at Corinth insulted Paul and greeted his message with blasphemy (cf. 18:6), so he once more announced (cf. 13:46) that he was turning to the Gentiles. God does not always call us to continue to deal with men who violently refuse our witness, though we must not be too quick to turn away from someone who might be won to Christ by patient and persevering love.

Paul left the synagogue, but he didn't go far. He started holding services in the home of Titus Justus, who lived next door. The leader of the synagogue, Crispus, became a Christian there. How this must have annoyed the Jews! (It is believed that Justus' full name was Gaius Titus Justus, and that he is the Gaius mentioned in Paul's letter to the Romans (16:23), which he wrote from Corinth on a later visit there.)

"Paul had not been sad when things looked much more hopeless. But though now he and his friends had many converts (Acts 18:8), some mood of sadness crept over him. Possibly he had reason to suspect that his very success had sharpened hostility, and to anticipate danger to his life" (Maclarin).

In any case, the Lord appeared to Paul at night in a vision and said, "Have no fear, but speak and do not keep still, because I am with you" (vv. 9, 10, BERK).

The comforting words, "Don't be afraid," have given new strength to God's workers in all ages. And it is not only physical harm we fear. Failure, domestic or financial problems may threaten.

But Jesus is with us. No Christian, be he pastor, missionary, policeman, fireman, miner, or construction worker, need "go it alone." God is well able to protect His people. In Paul's case, the promise was literally fulfilled in the failure of the attack described in verses 12-17.

Encouraged by the vision, Paul stayed on in Corinth for a year and a half (v. 11). While there, he wrote his two epistles to Thessalonica.

Hailed into Court

Gallio (v. 12), who became pro-consul of Achaia, or Southern Greece, of which Corinth was the capital, was a brother of Seneca, the famous Roman statesman. Gallio was free from petty personal considerations. The Corinthian Jews, "with one accord, rose up against Paul" and dragged him into court before Gallio, charging that the apostle was persuading men to worship contrary to Roman law (v. 13).

Bringing Paul before Gallio was a new step in Jewish opposition, which previously had been limited to inciting riots and bringing the apostles before minor magistrates. In Corinth, Paul was hailed for the first time before a superior tribunal.

But Gallio threw the case out of court as not coming under his jurisdiction.

"If the defendant had committed some crime," he said, in effect, "I would be glad to proceed, but I'm not interested in a dispute over words and names and Jewish traditions. Settle it yourselves!" And he expelled them (v. 16), thinking Christianity was simply a new Jewish sect.

We can't admire Gallio's inability to grasp spiritual distinctives, but his decision was an important one for Paul and the Gospel. It set a precedent for at least 10 years for other Roman governors to follow, and it showed Paul that he could rely on the Roman government to protect his liberty as a Christian preacher.

Gallio's dismissal of the charges against Paul was the signal for the Corinthian Greeks to stage a demonstration against the Jews. The apostle's would-be persecutor, Sosthenes, who had succeeded Crispus as synagogue leader, was manhandled by the crowd. The Gentiles had no love for the Hebrews. This episode shows how strong anti-semitism was even in those days. But the disorder left Gallio unmoved (v. 17). Perhaps he felt that Sosthenes was only getting what he deserved for bringing such a case into court.

"Many days" (v. 18) after the Gallio affair, Paul left Corinth, taking Aquila and Priscilla with him and leaving behind Timothy and Silas (who is not mentioned again in The Acts). Paul went on to Ephesus, but visited a barber in Cenchrea to have his hair cut, for "he was keeping a vow" (v. 18).

Paul has been severely criticized for this vow. Some feel that by it he compromised his conviction that since the death of Christ, the Mosaic ceremonial law no longer applied.

But this vow was simply another instance of Paul's becoming "all things to all men" so that he might bring them to Christ (1 Cor. 9:19-23). Working as he did among the Jews, Paul was willing to accommodate himself, within reason, to their ways. As we have seen previously, Paul's God was *not* "too small." The apostle did not conceive of the Lord as being limited by the strictures men put on Him. He knew that God is free to disregard any such rules.

But there *are* limits to how far one may go in "accommodating." A person who makes a practice of saying nothing about his personal faith lest he offend his business and/or social associates is not "accommodating." He is compromising.

Paul left Priscilla and Aquila in Ephesus, a flourishing city which was the site of the famed temple of Diana, or Artemis, one of the architectural wonders of the ancient world. (The King James Version of the Bible puts Aquila's name first because he was the husband, but Priscilla is usually named first in the Greek and was probably the more active of the two.)

The Jews at Ephesus wanted Paul to stay there longer, but he was in a hurry to get to Jerusalem, perhaps to celebrate the Passover, which that year came early in April. The Mediterranean was not normally open to navigation in the spring until March 10, and a sea voyage was a slow and precarious project at best, so Paul told the Ephesians he must not linger. He would return later if it were God's will (v. 21). All his plans were subject to the Lord's approval and modification, even if he did not use the phrase, "Lord willing," as glibly as some Christians do today.

Mission Completed

On reaching Caesarea, Paul traveled to Jerusalem to pay his respects to the Christians there. Then he went to Antioch, so completing his second missionary journey. He started his third journey almost at once (v. 23).

Meanwhile, Apollos had come to Ephesus from Egypt shortly after Paul left. He was a well-educated man, a gifted speaker, and an enthusiastic preacher. He was "mighty in the Scriptures" (v. 24), but was "acquainted only with the baptism of John" (v. 25). His knowledge of God's revelation was incomplete.

Apollos, it seems, was still preaching John's message, "Repent, for the kingdom of heaven is at hand." Apparently he had not heard or didn't understand the meaning of Jesus' atoning death and bodily resurrection. In these days of radio and television, such lack of communication appalls us. John The Baptist had been dead 25 years!

When Priscilla and Aquila heard Apollos preach, they did not embarrass him by correcting him in the public service. They took him aside afterward—perhaps inviting him to their home for a meal—and brought his theology up to date.

If you have ever tried to make a few suggestions to an organist, song leader, Sunday School teacher, or preacher, you know how touchy many Christians are. Any unfavorable comment on what they are doing may be taken as a stinging personal insult justifying their walking off their jobs in a huff.

Apollos, however, was a man of larger dimensions. He listened graciously to his friendly critics and thanked them, you may be sure, for their help. What is more, he took their advice and changed his message accordingly.

When Apollos decided to go to southern Greece (Achaia), the disciples encouraged him, writing letters to introduce him to the Christians there. On his arrival in Corinth, "he greatly helped those who had believed" (v. 27).

As one studies The Acts, it is impossible to avoid the impression that Paul and his associates in the Gospel ministry were energetically "on the go" for Christ. They had little time for rest and no time at all for self-pity. Their personal financial fortunes were of little concern to them. They appear to have been entirely lacking in what some today call "ambition." They were disinterested in ease, comfortable homes, popularity, and the other goals for which men have often worked so hard. Their one objective, at which they worked constantly, was to make Christ known, both to Jews and to Gentiles, as Saviour and coming Lord.

The typical Protestant church of the twentieth century could learn a good deal from the way our early Christian brothers did it!

18
Facing
a Riot

Acts 19

A good many Christians today are what has been called the sit, soak, and sour variety. They come to church and sit through sermon after sermon, soaking up sound, orthodox teaching. But instead of "translating" their learning into living, they actually do little or nothing about what they have heard. And so they "sour."

By this time, you will have observed that the first century Christians were of a somewhat different breed. They received the Gospel eagerly, and it made a practical difference in the way they lived and how they looked at life. Everything they were and did was affected by the wonderful truth that Christ had died for them, had risen from the dead, and was coming again.

Acts 19 is a particularly lively chapter, dealing as it does with the first part of Paul's third and last missionary journey, which took him again to Asia Minor and Greece. Luke does not give us a detailed account, but the Holy Spirit led him to record three or four colorful "cameos" of the exciting events that took place.

• Not long after completing his second journey, Paul set out once more (18:23) to encourage the Christians in the churches he had started. He had been in Ephesus briefly before and had promised to return if possible (18:19-21), so Ephesus was the first stop on his third journey.

There he met a dozen men whom he questioned about their spiritual experience. He found that though they had been baptized with the "baptism unto repentance" of John the Baptist, they had not received, or even heard of, the Holy Spirit. Perhaps they had been followers of Apollos before Priscilla and Aquila had set him straight (18:24-26). They were *religious* men, but they were definitely not Christians, for they knew nothing about Christ's atoning death and resurrection and were not indwelt by the Holy Spirit (Rom. 8:9). The Holy Spirit is *the* difference between "religion" and Christianity. Many folks today who belong to "Christian" churches hardly know who the Holy Spirit is (cf. Acts 19:2).

The men put their trust in Christ and confessed their faith by allowing Paul to baptize them in Jesus' name. And as the apostle laid hands on them, they received the Spirit, spoke in tongues, and began prophesying.

Except for Pentecost, this is the second of only two episodes recorded in The Acts in which the coming of the Holy Spirit was said to be attended by speaking in tongues. The other occasion was in the home of Cornelius (10:46), when Peter first "officially" preached the Gospel to Gentiles. Normally, neither the laying on of hands nor speaking in tongues attended the reception of the Spirit. It is the Spirit who baptizes every new believer into Christ's body the Church. (1 Cor. 12:13).

Where the Fish Are

• Because Paul believed that the Gospel was "for the Jew first," he would go first to the synagogue when he reached a new town. He went where the Jews were, unlike some churches that seem to think it is an unsaved person's responsibility to go where the Gospel is being preached. If the Church today can learn anything from a study of The Acts, it is that God's people must take the message to the lost *where the lost are*. To put a sign, "Welcome, Sinners!" on the church door is hardly adequate.

Paul preached in the Ephesian synagogue for three months before the opposition got so stiff that he had to hire a hall. Then he began holding meetings in the lecture room of Tyrannus, using the facilities, according to one version, from 10 to 4 each day, perhaps while Tyrannus was on an extended noonday siesta. This was not the last time a new church got its start in a school building.

In Ephesus, Paul was a downtown noonday preacher, and probably he reached many Ephesian business people, shoppers, and tourists. In fact, "all who lived in Asia [the province in which Ephesus was located] heard the word of the Lord, both Jew and Greek" (v. 10).

Paul was not "preaching" so much as he was "*reasoning*" (v. 9). He was conducting *discussions*. He did not do all the talking, but encouraged questions, expressions of opinion, and testimonies. Preaching (one-way communication from pulpit to pew) is a powerful evangelistic weapon, but it is not the *only* way to convey the Gospel. A well-guided discussion gives listeners opportunity to participate actively in the learning process, and demonstrates that there are reasonable answers for questions people ask about the Gospel.

• One reason for Paul's success in Ephesus was the unusual number of miracles that God worked there through him, mostly the healing of the sick and the casting out of demons.

The Christians would cast out demons in the name of Jesus, but Jewish exorcists used incantations supposedly derived from Solomon. They believed the greatest power was in the not-to-be-spoken name of Jehovah. The pronunciation of this name was known only to the high priest. In reading the Scriptures, the people would substitute the name "Lord" (as in the AV) when they came to "JHVH" (the form in which God's name was given in Hebrew).

Seven sons of Sceva, a Jewish high priest, were in Ephesus while Paul was there. Impressed by his success in exorcism, they tried using Jesus' name on a demon. To their surprise, the demoniac turned on two of them, snarling, "I recognize Jesus and I know about Paul, but who are *you?*" He leaped on them, tore off their clothes, and bit and clawed them.

The power of God and the power of Satan are both to be reckoned with. Anyone who trifles with either is, spiritually, playing with highly charged wires. People come close to this sort of thing when they make a profession of faith just to please a loved one, or join a church for social or business reasons.

Interesting results followed the defeat of Sceva's sons. "Fear fell upon [all the people] and . . . many of those who had believed kept coming, confessing and disclosing their practices" (vv. 17, 18). These Christians had clung to the practice of magic even after they had been saved, but now they brought their scrolls and other paraphernalia to the marketplace for a great bonfire. Some $50,000 worth of the unholy trash was burned.

Barriers to Belief

Some "Christians" today are wedded to the daily horoscope, the ouija board, tarot cards, and other fortune-telling devices. But magic is not the chain that keeps most Christians from complete dedication. One great enemy of the faith today is *materialism,* and another is a false concept of what God requires. Many a Christian tells himself, "I want to live for God. I want Him to use me." But his choice of priorities clearly shows he is more interested in personal gain or personal pleasure. Others say, "I would live for God, but I must be *practical!* I have to provide for my family. I can't neglect my business." As if God didn't *know* that! As if God expected him to be impractical, careless, or negligent. There is no conflict between God's will for us as Christians and God's will for us as parents or citizens.

When Christians face God's demands honestly and submit to them, as the believers in Ephesus did with regard to their magic, they can expect revival. When they confess and forsake their sins, they can expect the sort of spiritual advance that took place in Ephesus (v. 20), where a strong local church developed.

• Ephesus was the site of the great Temple of Artemis, the Greek goddess of fertility, nature, and youth. In the King James Version the name Diana is used for the goddess.

Each May, folks would come to Ephesus from the surrounding countryside for the rites conducted at Artemis' temple, and many of them bought small silver images of the goddess as souvenirs or good-luck charms. From the manufacture of these images the silversmiths of the city earned a good living.

Demetrius (v. 24) was a sort of union leader. Calling a meeting of his fellow craftsmen, he reminded them that their livelihood depended on the image business, and observed that the numbers of people Paul was converting to Christianity was not helping them at all.

Men can always be touched by an appeal to their pocketbooks. When a man sees that *money* is involved, he knows the issue is important. What is bad for business obviously is to be opposed, regardless of its social, moral, ecological, or religious implications. Besides, Demetrius pointed out (to show that he wasn't entirely materialistic), the very honor of Artemis was threatened.

"Thus the argument proceeded from finances to faith," one commentator says. "It began with the hard facts of making a living and ended in a shower of religious stars."

Demetrius was too smart to launch a campaign against Paul, who had gained thousands of friends in the city. Instead, he instigated a crusade for Artemis.

His slogan, "Our prosperity depends upon this business" (cf. v. 25), is still a potent motive. It opposes good ecology and the preservation of our wilderness areas, for example. And think of the liquor interests—of the 30,000 lives lost on American highways each year in accidents due to drunken drivers. Think of the broken homes, the blighted hopes, the wrecked lives. But the liquor interests are allowed to advertise their poison freely in our magazines. This privilege is not given the pushers of narcotics. Alcohol is as serious a moral issue as narcotics, and God's people ought to do all they can to fight both.

Nothing stirs people into a frenzy like a religious appeal based on practical business principles. Demetrius combined economics, religion, and patriotism. No wonder all Ephesus was filled with confusion as its citizens shrieked, "Great is Artemis of the Ephesians!" (v. 28)

The craftsmen, milling about in the streets, forced two of the apostle's associates into the amphitheatre, a magnificent structure (recently excavated) which seated 25,000 persons. Paul wanted to share the danger with his fellow workers, but they and the local officials (vv. 30, 31) would not allow him to do so.

Wild confusion prevailed in the amphitheater. Most of those present did not even know why they were there (v. 32). One person cried out one thing and another something else. When Alexander, one of the Jews present, saw that a riot was developing, he tried to make a public statement exonerating his people, but the crowd broke into a frenzy when they saw him. They knew that Jews as well as Christians opposed idolatry. The mob began shouting, over and over again, like a group of irresponsible adolescents, "Great is Artemis of the Ephesians!" (v. 34)

Cheers for the Clerk!

Demetrius had used his influence to start a riot, but the town clerk of Ephesus, a sort of middleman between the free rulers of the city and the Roman government, used *his* influence to stop it.

After the mob had worked off its emotions by

screaming for two whole hours, the town clerk mounted the rostrum and somehow quieted the crowd. Then he reasoned with them, and his arguments are worthy of study:

• The people were foolish to shout themselves hoarse about what everyone knew was "true." The world realized that Ephesus was temple warden of Artemis (cf. v. 35). And since the image of Artemis came down from heaven (it was probably a meteorite that roughly resembled a human body), it obviously was *not* among the gods whom Paul had attacked as "made with hands" (cf. v. 26).

• Paul and his associates had neither tried to rob the temple nor to blaspheme the goddess (v. 37). Had Paul used sarcasm, or openly attacked Artemis, in his speaking, he might have hopelessly antagonized those he wanted to win. We must never condone error, but by presenting the truth *positively* we often enable our hearers to see for themselves the folly of their false beliefs.

• If Demetrius and his followers had a just complaint, they should take regular legal action and bring charges against Paul in the courts, which were then in session (v. 38).

• If the people had other matters to settle or questions to ask, they should do so at a regular lawful assembly. Such meetings were held three times a month. The present gathering was not a meeting—it was a mob. The real danger, said the town clerk, was not so much loss of trade (cf. v. 27) as an investigation by the Romans (v. 40), who were not minded to tolerate riots.

The town clerk's reasonable words sobered the people, and after he had dismissed them, they went quietly back to their homes and places of business.

19
Warning: Wolves!

Acts 20

A sense of urgency—a feeling that the time is short—has come over Christians in recent years. Many are convinced that whatever God's people do not do *now* will not be done at all.

The Apostle Paul had this feeling, too, in the latter part of his ministry. It is reflected in the remaining chapters of The Acts.

Paul had been in Ephesus about three years (20:31), but toward the close of that time he had been convinced that his work there was finished (19:21). He wanted to return to Jerusalem and set out for Rome. As if in sympathy with his sense of urgency, Luke's account, in Acts 20, becomes quite sketchy.

Paul left Ephesus after the riot there, and traveled to Macedonia, or northern Greece. The phrase, "when he had gone through those districts" (20:2), suggests that he retraced the route of his second missionary journey, revisiting the churches in Philippi, Thessalonica, and Berea. Romans 15:19 indicates that he also traveled to the borders of Illyricum (modern Albania and Yugoslavia). We are not told, in The Acts, that as Paul traveled he and his associates received offerings for poor Christians in Jerusalem, but we piece this information together from other parts of the New Testament. Nor do we read here about Paul's concern over the trouble in the church at Corinth. He may have written his second letter to Corinth while in Macedonia on this second trip.

From Macedonia, Paul came down to Achaia (here called "Greece"), from where he wrote his epistle to the Romans.

The apostle was going to sail to Syria, but a Jewish plot, perhaps to sink his ship or to throw him overboard, caused him to return to Macedonia overland, and to embark for Syria from there (v. 3).

He spent a week at Troas, perhaps waiting for a ship. On Sunday evening, he met with the disciples there for a communion service (v. 7). This verse, and many others like it, disprove the Seventh Day Adventist claim that the early Christians met on Saturdays. It is true that they preached the Gospel in the synagogues on Saturdays, the day when the Jews were there, but the services of the Church were held on Sundays.

If your pastor has poor "terminal facilities," you will sympathize with Paul's audience at Troas. The meeting was held in a third-floor room. The air was murky because of the many lighted lamps and the number of people present, and Paul "prolonged his message until midnight" (v. 7). His heart was warm and full, his audience was eager to hear, and he was leaving in the morning.

Falling asleep in church is more a habit of age than of youth, but it was a young man, Eutychus, who dropped off at this meeting. Unfortunately, he had not picked his window seat with this event in mind, and he was apparently killed when he fell to the ground from the sill on which he had perched. He revived, however, as Paul held him.

Anxious to get on to Jerusalem, Paul had no time to stop in Ephesus, but since he did touch at Miletus, 30 miles away, he asked the elders of the Ephesian church to meet with him there.

Moving Message

Paul's farewell to these elders (vv. 18-35) is one of the most poignant addresses in the whole Bible. It is the only recorded sermon of Paul's delivered to an all-Christian audience. It lays bare the loving heart and the selfless life of one to whom the Lord Jesus and His Gospel were all that mattered. As you would expect, it is definitely not an "evangelistic" appeal.

Paul was not ashamed to speak of his own life and work (v. 18). He was not boasting, for he knew that he was what he was only because Christ lived in him. His humility (v. 19) grew out of the realization that he was merely an instrument in the Lord's hands. He did not look on his ministry as "a highly respected profession which gives one status," but as a bondservice in which he was Christ's slave.

Paul mentioned the two kinds of teaching he had done at Ephesus—"publicly and from house to house" (v. 20). The apostle knew the supreme importance of visitation, and though he had earned his living (v. 34) by making tents, he managed to *make* time to visit in homes and talk to people personally about repentance toward God, faith in the Lord Jesus Christ (v. 21), and growth toward spiritual maturity. The home Bible class movement, now gaining tremendously in popularity, is a variation of this type of ministry.

Paul spoke of his great sense of urgency (v. 22). He felt constrained to go to Jerusalem, though the Holy Spirit had been warning him that imprisonment and trouble waited for him there. Paul never needlessly courted danger (e.g., v. 3). However, the Spirit had not forbidden his going to Jerusalem (contra 16:6, 7), and he believed that to go was God's will. All he wanted of life was to finish the course God had given him (v. 24).

The apostle had yielded more than once to appeals from the brethren that he save himself from danger (e.g., 17:10; 19:30), but now such appeals had no effect. He *knew* this journey was God's will, and to lengthen his life by turning back from it was something he could not do. He was "expendable" in the Lord's service.

Paul was certain that he was bidding his Christian friends from Ephesus a last farewell (20:25), and as he reviewed his work among them he had no regrets. He was innocent of the blood of all men (v. 26). A Christian, like a prophet, is a watchman (Ezek. 3:17-21). One of his functions is to warn people of coming judgment. If he fails to do so, he shares some responsibility for those who are lost in sin. Paul had witnessed faithfully throughout his ministry.

"I did not shrink," he said, "from declaring to you the whole purpose of God." "Shrink" is a nautical term; it means to take in sail. Some people are willing to talk about Christ when the circumstances are right, but if there is any likelihood of embarrassment or ridicule, they "take in sail" and keep their mouths shut. This was not Paul's way. Even when it was not easy to confront men with the Gospel, and it would have been much simpler to say nothing, Paul spoke his piece.

Didn't Ride Hobbies

Preachers and teachers are sometimes tempted to "ride hobbies" instead of giving their people a "balanced diet." One minister preached through The Revelation three times in eight years. Some teachers sound as though the Holy Spirit were the only really important doctrine in Scripture. Or a church emphasizes evangelism at the expense of the spiritual development of believers. Another congregation may seldom hear an evangelistic message. One church treats foreign missions as if nothing else mattered; in another, all one hears about is the youth work.

Paul gave his hearers a solemn warning of what the Church was facing. This section of the chapter is particularly timely now, for the same prospects confront the Church today.

"Be on guard *for yourselves*," he told the elders of the church at Ephesus, "and *for all the flock* among which the Holy Spirit has made you overseers. . . . I know that after my departure savage wolves will come in among you, not sparing the flock; and from among your own selves men will arise, speaking perverse things, to draw away the disciples after them" (vv. 28-30).

This grim prediction, looking forward to the invasion of the Church by false teachers from without and to apostasy among those within, has been abundantly fulfilled. The first "wolves" may have been the legalistic Judaizers who dogged Paul's footsteps. Down through the centuries, many other wolves have appeared. Some have been motivated by love for money, popularity, or social contacts. Others have introduced teachings completely incompatible with Scripture. Still others have "crept in unnoticed . . . ungodly persons who turn the grace of our God into licentiousness" (Jude 4).

Some professed believers, Paul foretold, would turn from the truth and spread error in the Church, leading many astray. The progress of false doctrine inside the Church is clearly traceable in the letters given through the Apostle John to the seven churches of Asia Minor (Rev. 2 and 3). The final flowering of this corrupt trend is seen in the hundreds of "Christian" churches today in which the New Testament Gospel is never proclaimed. Their preachers assume that everyone is already on his way to heaven, and they don't want to hurt any feelings by talking about "sin."

A good many Christians have no discernment of error. If a speaker uses a few evangelical cliches and is "sincere," they never suspect that anything is wrong. Other Christians, sad to say, are "witch-hunters" in their zeal to combat error. They smell false doctrine in all that comes their way and are constantly pointing the finger of suspicion at everyone outside their own circle. The letters that Christian workers receive from such self-appointed defenders of the faith would be amusing if the situation were not so sad.

It is not heresy, for example, to believe that the six days of Creation were not 24-hour periods. This is a matter of *interpretation*. It is not heresy to believe that the Rapture will occur during or after the Tribulation. That, too, is a matter of *interpretation*. Don't be quick to brand as false teachers those who do not interpret the Bible as you do in every detail.

Eternal Vigilance

But if the Church is to remain true, it will be at the price of intelligent and continuing vigilance (v. 31). In spite of all efforts to safeguard Christian schools and pulpits against unbelief, false doctrine has often crept into and diverted whole denominations from the historic Christian position.

Paul did not take heresy lightly. "Always remember," he declared, with deep emotion, "that for three years, day and night, I never ceased warning you one by one, and that *with tears*" (v. 31, wms). If Christians don't shed tears today over false doctrine, it is only because they have no adequate conception of how serious its consequences are.

And now, as he was bringing to a close his work with these beloved converts, the apostle tenderly committed them to the Lord "and to the message of His favor, which is able to build you up and to give you your proper possession among all God's consecrated people" (v. 32, wms). He did not depend on their own watchfulness for their safe-keeping. He depended on God Himself, and on God's truth as contained in Scripture.

Christians face heresies, persecutions, and apostasy, but the cure for every spiritual ailment is the Word of God. If we are grounded in the Bible and its truth, we will not be easy victims for the grievous wolves Paul mentioned. Sad to say, however, thousands of Christians almost never study the Bible. Setting a wretched example for their children, they smile pityingly at the very idea that a full-grown man or woman would *study* a Sunday School lesson. They are usually willing to listen to sermons, tapes, and lessons, and to read books *about* the Bible, but as for actual Bible study . . . well, no, that's not their dish!

Fortunately, a strong trend *toward* Bible study is now developing!

In concluding his sermon, Paul reminded the Ephesians that he had accepted no salary for his work among them. "I have never coveted any man's silver or gold or clothes," he declared. "You know yourselves that these hands of mine"—and you can almost see his eloquent gesture—"provided for my own needs and for my companions [by making tents]. In everything I showed you that by working hard like this we must help those who are weak, and remember the words of the Lord Jesus, that He said, 'It makes one happier to give than to get.'" (vv. 33-35, wms)

That was the rule of Paul's life.

He knelt with his dear friends for a prayer of farewell. "There was loud weeping by them all, as they threw their arms around Paul's neck and kept on kissing him with affection" (v. 37, wms).

Isn't is regrettable that Christians today have for the most part given up revealing their Christian love in any visible form. Our handshakes are often as perfunctory as possible, and if anyone presumes to go beyond a handshake we tend to look askance at him. The believers of Paul's day were not so restrained. Who is to say they were not the richer for demonstrating the affection behind "the tie that binds our hearts in Christian love"?

20
Riot in
the Temple
Acts 21

On the following list, check the sources of your family's real friendships:

- *Neighbors*
- *Business associates*
- *Church contacts*
- *Christian activity (outside of church)*
- *Clubs or fraternal organizations*
- *Hobbies or sports interests*

Unlike other people, most evangelical believers find many of their friends among the fellow worshipers at their churches, though this is definitely not true in some less evangelical congregations. Most Roman Catholics will tell you frankly that they go to church to worship God and seldom find the church a source of friendships.

You have probably noticed, in reading through The Acts, how often there are suggestions that a warm spirit of camaraderie existed among first-century believers. We see this sort of love manifested when the elders of the church at Ephesus wept at Paul's departure and embraced him on the beach at Miletus (20:37). We see it in the loving concern Paul's friends had about his running into trouble in Jerusalem (21:4, 12). We see it in the open hospitality which Paul's party enjoyed in one place after another on their journey (vv. 4, 7, 8, 16), especially when the group came to Tyre. They looked up the Christian community there and, after only a week's stay, experienced such family feeling that all the local believers, men, women, and children, went to the beach with Paul and his associates (v. 5) and knelt and prayed with them there as they said goodbye.

The deep Christian love for each other among these early believers was noted by all who knew them, and genuine love for fellow Christians is still an evidence of eternal life and a ground for assurance (1 John 3:14). Unfortunately, many of us, like the church at Ephesus (Rev. 2:4), seem to have lost a good deal of the love that once characterized Christ's followers.

You may depend on it that the need for love is as great today as it ever was. In fact, in a culture which is becoming more and more automated and depersonalized, more persons than ever are turning to the Church of Christ looking for personal acceptance and friendship. More individuals than ever need access to the heart of Christian families, there to experience the love of God in all its healing, redemptive power.

Don't forget that if a person is to know the love of God it is not likely that he will experience it in any other way than through the words and actions of God's people. A kind word, an arm across one's shoulders, a practical bit of friendly caring—these can be far more encouraging than one might imagine.

The early part of Acts 21 details Paul's journey on his way to Jerusalem—from Miletus to Cos, then to Rhodes and Patara, then to Phoenicia and Tyre, and so on. Life is usually a series of "short hauls," taking us from where we are now to where, hopefully, God wants us to be tomorrow. Sometimes we travel on a non-stop flight, but more often the way-stops delay us annoyingly and remind us of a railroad trip, in the old days, on a milk train that stopped at every crossing.

Warned by Friends

At Tyre, Paul and his party sought out the local Christians. These believers warned him earnestly against continuing his journey to Jerusalem. Again, at Caesarea, he encountered more advice to avoid Jerusalem. The Prophet Agabus (cf. 11:28) gave a vivid object lesson predicting the apostle's imprisonment.

These Christians spoke "through the Spirit" (21: 4). That is, the Holy Spirit had impressed on them the fact that danger lay ahead for Paul. On this basis *they* (not the Spirit) strongly urged Paul not to go to Jerusalem.

Paul was a mature enough believer to know that God ordinarily gives His guidance directly to the person who is making a decision rather than to that person's friends or others. The Lord *may* use the advice of spiritual, mature, and experienced Christians in guiding us, but as a rule we must rely upon our own impressions of what He wants us to do.

Paul was well aware that trouble lay ahead (20:

23), and the tender concern of his friends almost broke his heart. In the end, though, his fellow Christians "fell silent, remarking, 'The will of the Lord be done!'" (21:14). No doubt God's purpose in all the warnings was not to deter Paul, but to prepare him. And while the apostle was in Jerusalem the Lord gave him a vision (23:11) that must have convinced him that he had done right in going up to the holy city.

Some Christians are like the man who tried to commit suicide by hanging himself with a rope tied around his waist. He found that when he put the rope around his neck it interfered with his breathing. Many a believer today is ready to "suffer and die" for Christ provided it doesn't hurt. Paul knew what going to Jerusalem would cost him, but did not allow this knowledge to turn him aside.

The Jerusalem believers received Paul with gladness (v. 17), but it may be significant that he was housed with Mnason, a disciple from way back, rather than with James, the Lord's half-brother, who was head of the Jerusalem church.

When Paul appeared before the elders, most commentators think, the atmosphere chilled somewhat. Jerusalem was the last great stronghold of legalistic Christianity. Gentiles were strong enough elsewhere to help break down the dividing wall (Eph. 2:14-18), but even the church's statement about circumcision and the law of Moses (chap. 15) had not wholly convinced the converted Pharisees.

Paul told the elders all the Lord had done through him (21:19), and they praised God and no doubt thanked Paul for the monetary gift he had brought from the Gentile churches of Greece and Asia.

"Yes, we praise God for all this wonderful work

among the Gentiles," the elders said, in effect, "but in the meantime, what about the *Jews* who believe? They are very zealous for the Law. They are disturbed to hear that you are telling other Jews, in Gentile areas, that they don't need to circumcise their sons or keep the ceremonial law or follow the cherished traditions of Judaism."

Clung to the Law

Remember that this confrontation took place some eight or nine years after the Council at Jerusalem had settled these issues. It is hard to understand the stubbornness of the Jewish Christians, but the law had been part of their very life for centuries. It was almost impossible for them to set it aside.

Paul urged believers not to allow themselves to be brought into bondage to the Law (Gal. 5:1). He himself, as Erdman puts it, "had rejected the Law as a means of justification, but not as a mode of life; he did not trust to its observance to secure his salvation, but he practiced its ceremonies as one who loved his nation and was glad to avoid giving needless offense to his fellow countrymen."

It isn't likely that the elders themselves believed the charges against Paul—and in any case, the rumors were not true. Paul *never* denied the right of Jewish parents to circumcise their sons. In fact, Paul himself had Timothy circumcised (16:1-3) for the sake of the Jews at Lystra and Iconium. And as for not observing "the customs" (21:21), Paul had declared his liberty in the Gospel but had also declared that he would forego his liberty to avoid wounding brothers who had oversensitive consciences (1 Cor. 8).

"What is your duty, then?" (Acts 22:22, wms), the elders asked Paul.

They went on to propose a way by which he might convince his opponents that he had proper respect for the traditions still cherished by the Jewish Christians. They suggested that he join four Jewish Christian men who were completing a Nazarite vow. He was to undergo the prescribed rites of purification, to remain in the Temple with them to avoid further defilement, and to pay the expenses of the sacrifices (including three sheep for each man) which must be offered before the men under the vow could cut their hair.

Your conscience may rebel at the idea of animal sacrifice being offered by Christians so long after Christ's crucifixion, but remember that the transition from animal offerings was a slow one in the experience of Jewish believers. Some of them, in Jerusalem, still sacrificed animals occasionally until the destruction of the Temple (A.D. 70). However, they had their own Christian meetings, too, usually in homes, on the first day of the week.

Paul has been bitterly criticized for his action here, but apparently he felt that no really important principle was compromised. This was another instance of accommodation: "Unto the Jews I became as a Jew, that I might gain the Jews" (1 Cor. 9:20). Paul was sure God would not be displeased if he acted like a Jew, on this occasion, in order to win the Jews. Bruce suggests that Paul was entirely free of "that lower brand of consistency which has been called 'the virtue of small minds.'"

Paul was willing not only to suffer for others, but to accommodate himself to them. Are *we?* Or do we take the rigid position that others must adapt themselves to us and to our ways if we are going to communicate the Gospel to them? Are we willing to meet people where they are—to learn *their* interests, to understand *their* personal needs? Will we cultivate, for Jesus' sake, the friendship of those who lack entirely our Christian background, our evangelical way of expressing ourselves, our social and recreational patterns?

Paul went "all the way" so that he might win some. How "winsome" do unbelievers find *us?*

We must face the fact, however, that Paul's action got him into deep trouble. While he was in the Temple some Asian Jews recognized him and said he was the one who preached against the Law and the Temple (v. 28). They had seen him on the streets with Trophimus, a Gentile, and they falsely accused him of bringing Trophimus into the Temple, which would have been a capital offense. Even today, troublemakers will fabricate accusations out of whole cloth in their efforts to get God's servants into trouble with a church or other group.

City in Uproar

In no time, Jerusalem was in an uproar and the Temple court resembled a riot. Paul's accusers dragged him out of the Temple to the street. (It would have wounded their tender consciences to have murdered him in its holy precincts!)

Adjoining the Temple court was the Tower of Antonia, barracks of the Roman soldiers stationed in Jerusalem. The tower was connected with the court by a staircase. The soldier on duty reported the riot to Claudius Lysias (23:26), his tribune, or chief captain, who promptly rushed to the rescue just in time to save Paul's life.

The commanding officer ordered the apostle

bound with two chains and asked the crowd what crime he had committed. The crowd was too excited for Lysias to understand them, so he had Paul taken into the barracks. The apostle was carried up the staircase while the angry Jews shouted, "Away with him!" Their attitude reminds us of the shouts of the crowd, years earlier, when Jesus stood before Pilate.

Lysias mistook Paul for an Egyptian rabble-rouser who, not long before, had escaped into the desert, leaving his followers to be cut to pieces by the Roman soldiers. Imagine the tribune's surprise when Paul asked him, in excellent Greek, "May I say something to you?" (21:37)

Given permission to speak, Paul explained that he was a citizen of Tarsus and asked if he might address the crowd in the courtyard below the staircase. When he had been given the tribune's consent, Paul motioned to the people with his hand. When there was a great hush, he spoke to them "in the Hebrew tongue" (v. 40) in what turned out to be a vain attempt to justify himself.

21
Witnessing at Home

Acts 22

When did you last talk to someone about what Jesus Christ means to you?

How often do you try to "give away" your faith?

After you have witnessed, do you ever have the feeling that your testimony would have been more effective if you had presented it differently?

Paul's address to the Jews in the Temple court is an excellent illustration of the principles involved in giving an effective witness. Paul had just been rescued from death by the Roman soldiers. He was defending himself under the most difficult circumstances and before a hostile crowd (22:30, 31, 36). He had been given permission to speak by the Roman officer who had arrested him.

After Paul motioned to the crowd with his hand, the rioting subsided and there was a great hush.

If you had been Paul, what would you have said?

Would you have spoken "the plain, unvarnished truth"? This would undoubtedly have given you a great deal of satisfaction, but how long would your audience have listened?

How Paul Did It

• Paul started out by identifying with his hearers. He addressed them in terms of respect: "Brethren and fathers" (22:1), he said, indicating that he understood their point of view and was of their background. His ancestry and training were similar to theirs. This approach would reassure them.

• When Paul's audience heard that he was talking to them in "the Hebrew dialect" (v. 2, lit.), the Aramaic speech commonly used by the Palestinian Jews of that day, they were even more attentive. If we want people to listen, we must talk their language. We can't expect unsaved persons to understand and respond to the numerous words and phrases that evangelicals use so freely among themselves. For example, to many people "believe" means to accept as truth. They wonder what they need to be "saved" from. "Revival," to them, is an upturn in business. "Repent" means only to feel sorry for what you have done. And so on.

It is important to talk to people in words they clearly understand. It is not compromise for us to use terms that an unchurched person can grasp. And we must make the Bible, too, available to people in modern, everyday English. Even if we, like many older Christians, much prefer the King James Version, we should not insist that our children and others read God's Word in the language of almost 400 years ago.

• In no way did Paul attack or insult his hearers. He admitted that they were as sincere as he was (cf. v. 3). Instead of telling them how different he was from them, he reminded them of how much he was *like* them, and of how much he and they had in common. He could have said that he had been a Jew but had learned better—that what *he* had was far superior to the Jewish religion. Instead, he admitted that he had so heartily shared their position and zeal for God that he had persecuted Christians to the death (v. 4).

• We may cut ourselves off from those we talk with if we give the impression that we have *always* been believers. We should admit that we once shared the viewpoint of our listeners, even if we weren't engaged in deep-dish sinning before our conversion.

• Later, Paul wrote that he counted all his Jewish advantages as "rubbish" (Phil. 3:8) for the sake of his knowledge of Christ, but he did not voice this opinion to the Jerusalem Jews. If he had, they would have silenced him at once.

It makes little sense to say things we know will unnecessarily alienate the people to whom we witness: "Well, the teachings of *your* church simply don't line up with what the Bible says!"

We should postpone as long as we can, when we are witnessing, controversial matters such as baptism, denominations, hypocrites in the church, "questionable" amusements, etc.

Paul's listeners could understand how his fanaticism led him to attack Christians so fiercely (vv. 4, 5). They knew he was speaking the truth about his attitude, and they must have wondered what in the world had happened to change him so dramatically. This, he now prepared to tell them.

• In his testimony, Paul spoke about himself, but he made plain the place Christ had in his conversion. He was not like the young woman who had talked incessantly about herself to her escort and who finally said, "Now let's talk about *you*—how do you like my dress?" We must feature Christ, not ourselves, in our witnessing.

Paul's conversion was not a gradual one. He could tell exactly where he was and the hour of the day when it happened (v. 6). There was no mistaking the identity of the One who spoke to him, and he did not hold back this truth from the angry Jews (vv. 7-9). He did not tell them, however, that Jesus had predicted his great sufferings (9:16). Most of Paul's afflictions had come from the Jews. It would have been satisfying to him to say that God had foretold their harshness, but doing so would have served no purpose.

• Paul had made it plain, up to this point, that his conversion did not involve a complete break with the Jews. He had done nothing contrary to the law of Moses. He accepted the pattern of the Old Testament.

Then he pointed out that Ananias (22:12), who had befriended him in Damascus, was a "devout" Jew. Like thousands of Christians in Jerusalem, Ananias observed the customs and traditions he had learned in his youth—such, perhaps, as synagogue worship and journeys to the Temple at Jerusalem on feast days. Paul himself observed the latter (20:16). Many Christians count it a special privilege, even today, to be in Bethlehem on Christmas Eve or in Jerusalem at Easter.

• Keep in mind that Paul's objective was to tell how God had changed the course of his life, and to do so without offending his hearers any more than necessary. That is why he used Hebrew terms for God ("the God of our fathers") and for Christ ("that Just One," av), and why he made it clear that he had been helped on his new course by Ananias, a godly *Jew*. And in telling about his divine commission as communicated to him by Ananias (9:15, 16; cf. Gal. 1:1, 12), Paul used the term "all men" instead of "Gentiles." He knew that the latter word would offend his hearers.

• Paul did not mention, in his defense, that Ananias was a Christian. This omission was not deceit. It was plain common sense. We must never tell a lie, but we don't always need to tell everything we know.

• The scope of Paul's witness was to be what he had seen and heard (Acts 22:15). This is to be the scope of every Christian's testimony. What has God done for, in, and through *you* lately? Perhaps the reason so many professing Christians have little or nothing to say for Christ is that they have little or no personal experience with the power and grace of God. When Christians are driven to telling what God is doing for someone else, or what God did for them *23 years ago*, their testimony is not nearly as effective as when they can talk about how He is presently active in their lives.

• Paul omitted any reference to the time he had spent in Arabia (Gal. 1:17), but he told how after his conversion he did *not* go to the Gentiles, but to Jerusalem (Acts 22:17). There, while having his devotions *in the Temple*, he received the Lord's command to leave the city. He made it plain, in telling this, that he had not left Jerusalem because of any feeling against the Jews on his part.

God told Paul that his testimony would not be accepted by everyone. Because this is true of our witness, too, we must learn to be sensitive to the Holy Spirit's guidance as to whom we should speak to, lest we waste our time dealing with those whose hearts God has not prepared.

"Lead me to some soul today" ought to be our

prayer each morning of our lives, and then we ought to be on the alert to recognize the soul God leads us to. Our testimony must be tactful and sincere, but we can't expect always to win our prospect. *That* is the Holy Spirit's work. If we are faithful, loving, and tactful, God doesn't hold us responsible for the results.

• Paul had really "argued" with God about the order to leave Jerusalem (vv. 19, 20). He felt that his former animosity to Christians would make his testimony to the Jews more effective. But God had other plans for him, and told him to go: "I will send you far away," said the Lord, "to the Gentiles" (v. 21).

• Paul had been as tactful as possible, but he would not be tactful at the expense of the truth. He had arranged his "material" in such a way as to give his hearers as much time as possible to hear his case. Now he must step on the toes of his audience and admit that he was involved in evangelizing the Gentiles, whom they despised.

Explosion

The Jews in Jerusalem might have tolerated a Jewish Christian church as a sect of Judaism, but a church composed of both Jews and uncircumcised Gentiles was an abomination of Israel. As soon as the word "Gentiles" escaped Paul's lips, his audience went wild with uncontrolled hatred and started screaming for the apostle's death.

This sort of prejudice against those of an "inferior" (i.e., different) group is still all too prevalent. In some gatherings of professing believers, one needs only to mention "racism" to have the temperature drop 10 degrees.

Paul finally told the full truth, even though he must have strongly suspected it would cost him his audience. Many believers, in their desire to witness tactfully, *never* get to the point—and *that* fault is as bad as, or worse than, being too blunt and alienating people by premature directness or poor taste. A testimony that never gets around to the "unpalatable truth" is worthless. We must not only he tactful but faithful. Paul was.

The startled Roman officer probably couldn't comprehend what the pandemonium in the Temple court was about. Perhaps he hadn't understood Paul's Aramaic testimony. He ordered the prisoner taken into the castle and scourged so that, under this "third degree," he might confess. Scourging, as the Romans practiced it, was a murderous punishment. Many men died undergoing it.

Paul was scourged five times, was beaten three times with rods, and on at least one occasion was stoned (2 Cor. 11:23-25). He knew, however, that there is no sense in suffering for suffering's sake. He knew what some Christians do not seem to have learned—that martyrdom is of value only when it cannot be avoided with integrity. "A cheap martyrdom never produces any great result."

So the apostle told the soldiers, who were strapping him in preparation for flogging, that he was a Roman citizen. As such, he was exempt from scourging. When the tribune heard this news, he was afraid he would get into trouble for having abused a Roman.

We don't know just how Paul proved his citizenship, but on this occasion it spared him much suffering.

Perhaps the commander was being sarcastic when he commented to Paul that *his* citizenship had cost him a pretty penny (v. 28). "The price must have come down," he perhaps implied, "if someone like *you* can afford it!"

But Paul had the last word.

"I didn't buy it—I was *born* a citizen," he said quietly.

The next day Lysias ordered the Jewish Sanhedrin to assemble and to try Paul (v. 30).

One interesting question must be raised concerning this chapter and the rest of The Acts.

Where were the Christians of Jerusalem?

The Christian church, to which Paul had reported on his arrival in the city (21:18), must have heard about the riot in the Temple. The four Christian Jews whose expenses Paul had paid (21:26, 27) would surely have reported the apostle's predicament to James, the leader of the church. But from this time until Paul left for Rome two years later, we have no record of the Jerusalem believers doing anything to help or encourage him.

One must not argue dogmatically from the silence of so fragmentary and selective a record, but one gets the impression that the Jewish Christians of Jerusalem washed their hands of Paul and remained discreetly in the background.

We hope this was not really the case!

22
In Times of Crisis

Acts 23

While Paul was in Ephesus, he had reached a settled conclusion that his ministry would not be complete until he had preached in Rome (19:21). He planned, at that time, to return first to Jerusalem, delivering to the poor saints there the money contributed by the churches of northern and perhaps southern Greece. He was warned frequently, en route to the holy city, that serious trouble would come from his going there, and we have seen how true these predictions were. Paul must have been tempted to wonder whether or not his determination to go up to Jerusalem had been a mistake.

Chapter 23 is one of the most exciting portions of The Acts. It tells us how God guided the apostle in a time of great crisis, how the Lord confirmed Paul's conviction that he must go to Jerusalem, and how He used a combination of adverse circumstances to take the apostle to Rome, the world capital—at government expense.

Claudius Lysias, tribune of the Roman troops at the Tower of Antonia, kept Paul in chains overnight, after his arrest, though he had spared him a scourging because he was a Roman citizen. The next day, because he was so eager to learn what the Jews had against Paul, Lysias ordered the Sanhedrin to assemble (22:30) and give Paul a hearing.

Short Session

The trial got off to an exciting start, but it was over almost before it began.

Because Paul was a Pharisee (many Pharisees had become Christians), he addressed the Sanhedrin as an equal (23:1). He began by observing that his conscience was clear (cf. 24:16). A conscience enlightened by the Holy Spirit is an excellent moral guide, but an unenlightened conscience can be sadly in error. Back in the days when he was persecuting Christians, Paul's conscience had also been clear—but mistaken.

Paul's claim was too much for Ananias, the high priest, who has been described as a notoriously unscrupulous and avaricious politician. He ordered someone standing near Paul to strike him across the mouth, a form of rebuke common among the Jews.

Paul's reaction was immediate and violent.

"God is going to strike you, you whitewashed wall!" he said. "Do you sit to try me according to the Law, and in violation of the Law order me to be struck?" (v. 3)

Jewish law presumed a person innocent until he had been found guilty. Paul had a right to object to this blow, but under similar circumstances (John 18:19-23) the Lord Jesus spoke far less impulsively. Paul was a human being and was under terrific tension. He deserves our patient understanding. His statement, too, was more of a prediction than a curse. A few years later, says Josephus, the secular

Jewish historian, assassins dragged Ananias out of a sewer and murdered him.

"Do you dare to revile God's high priest?" one of the bystanders asked Paul.

"I realize that one must not speak evil of a ruler," said Paul, "but I didn't know this man was the high priest."

Paul's apology, if such it can be called, was accompanied by a sort of justification for what he had done. Some think that because the high priesthood changed hands often, Paul had not met Ananias in his official capacity, or did not recognize him. Perhaps he was not wearing his robes of office. Some think Paul had poor vision (cf. "looking intently," v. 1) and did not see who had given the order to strike him. And some would paraphrase what he said: "I couldn't believe that any man who gave an order like that could be the high priest!"

Officeholders who abuse their positions or use them to defraud the people or to gratify their personal whims forfeit their right to any personal respect from those they "serve."

Sometimes, however, we must honor a man's position even if we cannot honor the man. Ungodly men are likely to "despise dominion and speak evil of dignities" (Jude 8, AV). As an illustration, Jude mentions a dispute between Michael the archangel and Satan (Jude 9), and emphasizes that Michael did not dare bring a railing accusation against the devil, who still has a high position in the universe by virtue of which he is still held in respect by the heavenly hosts.

Disrespect is common wherever men enjoy liberty of speech. Those who hold the highest offices in our land do not escape it, for we find it easy to "despise dominion." Protestants especially may feel free to speak with contempt about church officers and pastors. And we seldom concern ourselves about how near we come to holding spiritual powers in contempt with our flippant talk about Satan or about the angels.

Stroke of Genius

The quick blow that had followed Paul's opening remark convinced the apostle that he had no chance of getting a fair hearing and that his trial would be as much a farce as our Lord's. As he looked around and saw that the Council was made up of both Pharisees and Sadducees, a sudden idea flashed through his mind.

The Sadducees were "humanists." They accepted nothing of the supernatural (v. 8). They did not believe in a future life, in angels or demons, or in miracles. They were the custodians of the Temple, a lucrative enterprise which they wanted at all costs to preserve.

The Pharisees, on the other hand, accepted the supernatural, and not all of them were hypocrites. Many, like Paul himself, had been converted by the Gospel. A Pharisee could become a Christian and still be a Pharisee, but no one could at the same time be a Christian and a Sadducee.

Noticing these two groups, with their distinctive garments, Paul shouted, "I am a Pharisee, a son of Pharisees; I am on trial for the hope and resurrection of the dead!" (v. 6)

The effect was more than the apostle had hoped. The Pharisees and the Sadducees began at once to argue with each other about the resurrection, probably with much heat. Some of the Pharisees, who had been eager to see Paul put to death, started to shout, "We find nothing wrong with this man; suppose a spirit or an angel has spoken to him?"

So fierce was the dissension that developed that Paul was in the position of a worm whose ends are in the beaks of two chickens. The tribune, afraid the two factions would tear the apostle apart, ordered the soldiers to bring him back into the barracks.

Some commentators think Paul's tactics here were a bit of human shrewdness and not quite worthy, spiritually, of the occasion. Perhaps so, but Paul could also have been acting under the leading of the Holy Spirit.

You can expect guidance in an emergency, when there is no time to pray, as well as in the face of a long-standing problem saturated with intercession. The secret of such on-the-spot guidance is to live in constant obedience to God, to keep your sins confessed, and to *expect* God to direct you. If these things are true and you make a spontaneous decision, you may be sure you are acting in God's will.

Church Division

We smile at the division in the Sanhedrin, but division in the church today is nothing to smile about. When members of a local church are constantly bickering, and when some even leave over small differences and organize a competing evangelical church in the same community, how can the Church hope to have a strong witness in that area? How can unregenerate people get a favorable impression of this kind of "Christianity"?

Throughout her history, the Church has been

torn by schisms of one kind or another. One can accept these divisions when they result from real doctrinal differences, but all too often they grow out of petty clashes and unreasonable dogmatism between individuals.

We have noted that members of the church in Jerusalem appear to have left Paul alone, but he was not without a Comforter. The next night the Lord Himself stood at His servant's side.

"Take courage, for as you have solemnly witnessed to My cause at Jerusalem, so you must witness at Rome also" (v. 11), said Jesus.

This vision must have been like balm from Gilead to Paul. Perhaps he had been wondering whether he shouldn't have stayed away from Jerusalem after all. Certainly the apparent results of his visit were nil.

But the Lord judges His servants by their faithfulness (1 Cor. 4:2) rather than by statistics. He didn't rebuke His tired and discouraged apostle, seemingly deserted by his own companions. "Be of good cheer," Jesus told Paul, reassuring Him that he would have the dear wish of his heart, the privilege of preaching the Gospel in Rome.

The fulfillment of God's promise that Paul would get to Rome took a long time. Many weary months of imprisonment and difficulty intervened. Just as many an American youth, unable to afford travel abroad, has seen the world after joining the Navy or the Marines, so Paul would get to Rome at last—at the expense of the Roman government.

Meanwhile, some 40 Jews banded together and vowed neither to eat nor drink until they had killed Paul. They planned to have the Sanhedrin ask the tribune to bring Paul into court again in the morning, and to waylay him and kill him en route.

The plot was discovered by Paul's nephew, apparently a young teen-ager (cf. "by the hand," v. 19). We have no way of knowing how he learned what was going on, except that boys have a way of getting into all sorts of places and learning all kinds of secrets. Perhaps the father of one of his friends was a Pharisee, or he had overheard some of the plotters while hanging around the Temple court. We don't know, either, how the boy was able to visit his Uncle Paul, except that as a Roman citizen the apostle may not have been closely confined. In any case, Paul was alerted to his danger.

Small Boy Used

Sometimes God acts miraculously, as when He released Peter from prison (12:7), but much more frequently He uses human beings. Here He used a small boy.

When the boy told Paul about the plot, Paul didn't say, "Sonny, let's ask the Lord to frustrate the schemes of these wicked men!" The apostle no doubt prayed, but he did more than pray. He took what action seemed logical and right under the circumstances. He used common sense. He sent the boy to the tribune to report the plot, and Claudius Lysias made immediate plans to transfer Paul to safety that very night, in the company of nearly 500 troops.

How the conspirators must have gnashed their teeth when they learned, next day, what had happened! Fortunately for them, Jewish customs provided technicalities by which they could easily void their vow neither to eat nor drink until Paul was dead!

So the Apostle Paul made the first leg of his

trip to Rome with a guard of honor. The tribune sent him to Caesarea, the provincial capital of Judea at that time, in order to be tried there before Felix.

Felix, the governor of the province, was a man of unsavory character. Tacitus, the Roman historian, speaks of him as one who "in the practice of all kinds of lusts and cruelty . . . exercised the power of a king with the temper of a slave."

The message Lysias sent Felix with Paul is a study in the way men handle truth when they want to make the best possible personal impression.

"When this man was arrested by the Jews and was about to be slain by them," wrote Lysias, "I came upon them with the troops and rescued him, having learned that he was a Roman" (v. 27).

Actually, when Lysias first rescued Paul from the irate Jews in the Temple court, he had supposed the apostle to be a murderous Egyptian who had headed up a revolt of some 4,000 men (21:38). And he had not learned about Paul's Roman citizenship until after the apostle had been strapped preparatory to scourging, after Paul's address to the blood-thirsty mob.

Lysias' letter and the apostle were turned over to Felix, who declared that he would hear the case after the arrival of the defendant's accusers. Meanwhile, Paul was lodged in Herod's praetorium, probably in reasonably comfortable quarters.

23
Don't
Procrastinate!
Acts 24

A person confronted with the Gospel may respond in one of three ways. He may accept it, he may reject it, or he may postpone a decision. The last amounts to at least temporary rejection.

When you face *any* major decision—purchasing a house or a car, accepting a new job, or making a deeper commitment to God—postponement is always easy. When you make up your mind *not* to decide *right now*, you can stop thinking, for the time being, about your problem.

Felix, the Roman governor of Judea, is a classic example of procrastination and its effects. It was to him that Claudias Lysias sent the Apostle Paul after the latter's remark about the Resurrection had caused a near-riot in the Sanhedrin. Felix was not an ornament to the human race. He had been born a slave but had been given a political "plum" because his brother had influence.

Five days after Paul's arrival in Caesarea, Ananias, the high priest, came down from Jerusalem with a third-rate Roman lawyer, Tertullus, who presented the charges of the Jews against the apostle. Tertullus' speech "began with a magnificent flourish, but trailed away to a lame and impotent conclusion" (Bruce). He started by throwing orchids at the governor, thanking him for peace and quiet though actually his rule was characterized by injustice and bloodshed. Insincerity, about themselves or their hearers, is one of the great temptations people who do much public speaking must resist.

Making a Case

The preliminaries out of the way, Tertullus proceeded to indict Paul. He knew that Felix was concerned with the *political* and *social* aspects of the case rather than its *religious* side. He wanted to get Paul convicted as an offender against the Roman government. His charges were three in number (vv. 5, 6):

1. Paul was "a real pest . . . who stirs up dissension among all the Jews throughout the world." The apostle, he implied, was spreading discontent with the Roman government over the entire known world. One wonders that Felix did not suspect the motive behind such a charge, for the Jews had no loyalty to Rome. They hated the Romans and would have cheered anyone, even Paul, if he were opposing the imperial government.

2. Paul was a ringleader of the sect of the Nazarenes. The Romans did not interfere with those whose faith had been recognized as a "legal religion," but by referring to Christianity as a "heresy" (BERK), Tertullus branded it as an illegal threat to lawful religion and implied that the state should punish Paul.

3. Paul had desecrated the Temple by taking a

Gentile into its sacred courts (21:27-29). This charge was wholly false and was based on Paul's having been seen on the streets of Jerusalem with Trophimus, who was a Gentile. The Romans recognized desecration of the Temple as a crime worthy of death.

Having accused Paul of treason against Rome, schism against Moses, and sacrilege against the Temple, Tertullus brought his speech to an end, offering no shred of evidence to support his charges. Ananias and the Jews with him "joined in the attack" (v. 9), insisting that the lawyer had spoken the truth.

Pleading Not Guilty

Then it was Paul's turn. His opening remarks were respectful and courteous, but he did not stoop to flatter Felix. He took up each of the three charges against him:

1. As to his allegedly fomenting sedition, Paul pointed out that he arrived in Jerusalem only 12 days earlier (v. 11). He had been in Caesarea for five of those days, in the Tower of Antonia for two more, and in the Temple for several days with the men who had taken a vow (21:27). Obviously there had been no time in which he could have been stirring up trouble for the government! And nowhere had anyone seen him "disputing with any opponent or collecting a crowd" (v. 12, WEY).

2. As to his being a ringleader of the Nazarenes, Paul confessed that he worshiped God according to the way which his accusers called a sect (v. 14). But the God of Paul's fathers, whom he served, was the very God whom his accusers also worshiped. Not only did he believe in their God,

but he accepted "the Law and the prophets" in their entirety. He also believed in the resurrection (v. 15), in which the Pharisees believed. *His* religion, in fact, was that of the Jews carried to its logical and ultimate conclusion.

Paul was hinting strongly that if his accusers believed the Law and the prophets and were as convinced as he was about the resurrection (v. 13), they too would have become "Nazarenes."

His doctrinal beliefs, Paul went on to say, were more than a mere set of truths to which he gave mental assent: "In view of this [hope in God and belief in the resurrection], I do my best to maintain always a blameless conscience both before God and before men" (v. 16).

God intends that our beliefs constitute a basis for our lives. We are to live what we believe. And a conscience clear toward God *and toward men* is essential to an effective Christian testimony.

3. Paul went on to explain his presence in Jerusalem and in the Temple. He had come to the city to worship and to deliver monetary gifts from Macedonia for needy Jewish Christians (cf. 1 Cor. 16: 1-4; 2 Cor. 8 and 9; Rom. 15:26), and had presented sacrifices at the Temple (Acts 24:17). He was observing the Temple ordinances in a perfectly legitimate manner when certain Jews "from Asia" found him there and brought a false accusation against him (v. 18). It was they, not Paul, who had created the disturbance. *They* had stirred up the whole city and almost lynched the apostle. *They,* Paul pointed out, should have come to Caesarea to accuse him, for the Pharisees had admitted (23:9) that they found no fault in him.

Paul's defense is pretty well summarized in 24:13: "Nor can they prove to you the charges of which they now accuse me." The trumped-up accusations were entirely unsupported by evidence, and Paul flatly denied them. The only complaint he would allow was that at the meeting of the Sanhedrin he had shouted out that he was on trial because he believed in the resurrection of the dead (v. 21; cf. 23:6).

The apostle's accusers had nothing to say on this point. They knew very well that Rome would not execute or imprison a man for believing in the resurrection.

Felix realized that if he condemned Paul he would be perpetrating a grave miscarriage of Roman justice, for Paul was obviously innocent. However, if he released him he would offend the Jews, who hated the governor heartily and with whom he therefore wanted to gain favor. He decided to delay his decision. "Since he understood the teachings of the Way quite well, he adjourned the case" (24:22, BERK) pending the arrival of Lysias, whose testimony (23:26-30) he already had—in writing. So far as we know, Lysias never put in an appearance, and two years later Paul was still a captive.

Felix, faced with a thorny decision, chose the shameful way of postponement. He would settle Paul's case "tomorrow."

We sometimes poke fun unjustly at our Latin American neighbors. We picture them as easygoing people who, when faced with work, shrug comfortably as they mutter, "Mañana! Mañana!"

Actually, *mañana* (tomorrow) is all too common a word in our own vocabulary. We are often glad for any pretext to postpone until tomorrow, or next week, what we ought to be doing today, whether it is washing the car, cleaning a closet, or writing our will.

There are times when we *must* postpone making a decision. Sometimes we need to wait until we have acquired more information. Sometimes we need time to study the implications of what we are thinking of doing. Sometimes we must wait for God's leading, or to discuss our problem with someone who can advise us. There is no merit in being impetuous in making important decisions. But Felix had none of these reasons for delay. He was simply torn between expediency and duty, and so he postponed doing what he knew he ought to do.

Felix had persuaded Drusilla, who became his third wife, to leave her husband, the king of Emesa, and live with him. We can't be too sure just what prompted him to send for Paul so that the apostle might speak to him and Drusilla about his faith in Christ. Both members of this alliance were acquainted with Christianity, but their interest was purely academic. And no one ever gets to heaven merely by knowing what's in the Bible. A professor of Systematic Theology has no advantage over *you* when it comes to being a Christian. Salvation is a personal relationship to Jesus Christ, not mastery of a set of doctrinal propositions.

Timely Topics

Paul spoke to the royal couple about three matters (v. 25) that were highly relevant to them:

• *Righteousness.* Multitudes today believe they personally are more good than bad, and so deserve heaven. They need to be confronted with the fact that all our human righteousnesses are as filthy rags (Isa. 64:6) and that in Christ God provides the only righteousness (Rom. 3:22) that will satisfy Him.

Felix and Drusilla, both of them lustful and sinful, must have cringed as the apostle faced them with the holiness and purity of God.

• *Self-control.* Here, too, the royal couple must have squirmed. Many unregenerate people completely fail to restrain their appetites. Because Felix and Drusilla were rulers, they felt they could gratify every impulse of their natures. Many men and women today—particularly those with money—despise the idea of a God and do the same thing. Axioms of our day include, "If it feels good, do it"; and "Try it—you'll like it!"

• *Judgment.* Paul pointed out, no doubt, that God offers men full pardon and salvation on the basis of personal trust in Jesus Christ, but you may be sure he went on, in talking about "the judgment to come," to make it clear that the Lord will deal with the sin of all who reject His Son. A day of reckoning is ahead, and men will reap what they sow.

Felix was "terrified" (v. 25, ASV). "The Word discerned the thoughts and intents of his heart, but that heart even then clung to its idols" (Brown). Though conviction was gripping him and loosening the cords that bound him to his worldly pleasures, he resisted with all his power. In a tremendous effort of the will, he curtly dismissed Paul, saying, "You may go now. When I can spare the time I will send for you" (BERK).

Once more Felix's inclination to procrastinate proved his undoing. He had put off making a decision about Paul's guilt or innocence. Now, when confronted with a personal decision vastly more important, he again delayed. Once more he would not make a negative decision (reject the Gospel) because he knew it would be wrong, and he would not make a positive decision (turn from sin to Christ) because he did not want to pay the price. So he procrastinated, which was equivalent to saying "No!" to God.

Perhaps Felix's greed had mastered him. He had heard Paul mention the money he brought to Jerusalem (v. 17). Perhaps he thought Paul was still in possession of these funds, and expected the apostle to offer him a bribe. Whether he ever again came under conviction we do not know.

There are many motives for delay in coming to Christ. Some people delay because they want to have their "fling" first. Some want to concentrate on making money until they have all they think they will need. Some think such a decision would interfere with their business career or social contacts.

Procrastination is one of the devil's favorite tools. Satan doesn't insist that a person *reject* the Gospel—he is completely happy so long as an individual continues to postpone yielding to the Holy Spirit. He will convince you, if he can, that there is no hurry about breaking off that bad habit, starting to read the Bible regularly, or telling a neighbor about Christ.

And the sad truth is that by the time you realize that Satan has duped you, it may be too late for you to do much except regret your delay.

24
Who's on Trial?

Acts 25 and 26

If one lacks artistic training and discernment and knows nothing about painting, he would make a complete fool of himself if he undertook to criticize the pictures of Rembrandt, Vermeer, Reubens, and other famous artists.

Such masterpieces have proved their merit by enduring the test of time. They are no longer on trial. We may like them or dislike them, but our opinion does not affect their greatness one iota. We put ourselves on trial when we presume to sit in judgment on them.

Down through the ages, some men and women have presumed to sit in judgment on Christianity. They have held it up to scorn and ridicule and have even cursed it. But their contempt and their attacks have made no difference. Christianity is not on trial. Those who come into contact with it are.

The Apostle Paul was a man who was wholly dedicated to the service of God and his fellowman. His family, his training, his prestige—he counted all but rubbish compared with the knowledge of his Lord. His life was pure and selfless, and his greatest goal was to declare the Gospel to all men everywhere.

The VIPs who sat in judgment on Paul cannot stand when we compare them with him, as we have seen in recent chapters. It was they, not the apostle, who were really on trial.

Jewish Religious Leaders

The Hebrew hierarchy began to persecute Paul soon after his conversion, and when he returned to Jerusalem from his third missionary journey they made a determined effort, through the military power of Rome, to do away with him. They were not ready to end their opposition even after he had served two years in prison (24:27). Nothing less than his death would satisfy them.

The religious leaders had no valid complaint against Paul. He had done nothing they could legally condemn. He had observed the forms of the Law—not because they had any saving value but because he did not want to give needless offense (see e.g., 21:23-26). His very willingness to pacify the Jews who were critical of him was the thing that led to his being attacked by Jews while he was in the Temple worshiping according to the Law.

Every Roman official who heard the Jews' complaints against Paul threw their case out of court. Paul had done nothing worthy of punishment. Only Felix's desire to win the favor of the Jews (24:27) led him to keep Paul in confinement.

The caliber of Paul's Jewish opponents is plainly seen in their willingness to put the apostle to death by foul means if not by fair. They had plotted against him in Jerusalem (20:12) and in Caesarea (25:3), and only the protection of the Roman government enabled him to escape them.

Because of their knowledge of the Old Testament, and because of Jesus' open ministry among them and the many miracles He had performed, it is incredible that the Jews should not have recognized the Messiah proclaimed by Paul. The only valid explanation is that these Jews enjoyed the religious *status quo*, which gave them personal prestige and was extremely lucrative to them. They were ready to kill Paul because he threatened their position.

It is hard to escape the conclusion that these men were wilfully blind to the truth. There are always some people who close their minds to the Gospel because it would not be convenient for them to accept it. It would too radically affect their way of life.

Felix

We looked at this wretch in Acts 24. He is typical of people who are familiar with the facts of the Gospel. They can explain the plan of salvation, perhaps, but they themselves have never been born again. Their knowledge of the truth has never penetrated beyond their intellect. Knowledge of the Gospel leads to salvation only if one admits his sinfulness and trusts in the sacrificial, atoning death of the Lord Jesus Christ, the Lamb of God.

Perhaps Felix came close to doing this, but he put off making a binding decision and, so far as we know, never got around to doing it. He went out into eternity with life's greatest decision unmade.

Don't be satisfied to know *about* Christ without knowing *Him!* There's a world of difference!

Festus

This Roman took Felix's place as governor of Judea. Three days after he came into office he made a goodwill visit to Jerusalem (25:1). The Jews there, still hostile toward Paul, asked that the apostle be returned to Jerusalem to stand trial. They planned to ambush him and kill him on the way. But Festus insisted that they send their representatives to Caesarea, and this decision saved Paul's life.

At this trial, also, the Jews brought many serious charges, which they could not prove, against the apostle. Festus asked Paul if he would be willing to return to Jerusalem for trial, but Paul knew better than to trust himself to the Sanhedrin. He was standing trial in a Roman court (cf. v. 10), and since he had committed no crime against the Jews, he could not rightfully be turned over to them. He appealed his case to the emperor, Nero Augustus (v. 11).

Festus was pleased to have Paul off his hands, but he was a bit perplexed, too. He knew Paul was innocent, so on what basis could he send him to Rome? (cf. vv. 18, 19, 27)

When King Agrippa of Chalcis, a small kingdom north of Galilee, paid a courtesy call on the new governor, Festus was glad. Agrippa was a thorough student of Jewish religion, and might offer valuable advice. Festus arranged for Agrippa and Bernice, his mistress, to sit in on a hearing for Paul. He explained that the Jews' charges against the apostle involved unimportant religious details in which he himself was not at all interested.

Paul was always happy to present the Gospel. He told his three hearers about his strict Phari-

saical upbringing and said the Jews were persecuting him in spite of the fact that he believed the
same promise—that of the resurrection—which the
Pharisees also believed.

The apostle said he had once felt it his duty to
persecute Christians, and related once again his
miraculous conversion experience, when, on the
road to Damascus, the Lord Jesus had appeared
to him and commissioned him (26:16-18).

"I could not disobey that heavenly vision" (v.
19, wms), said Paul of this turning point in his
life. He went on to tell how he had ministered in
Damascus, in Jerusalem, around Judea, and then to
the Gentiles afar off, urging all men to repent and
believe. Because of this, he said, the Jews were
trying to kill him.

To Festus, Paul's words were the ravings of a
maniac. "You are crazy, Paul" (cf. v. 24), he declared emphatically. "Too much study has driven
you out of your mind!"

Festus is typical of people who sneer at those
who take Christianity seriously. These contemptu-
ous people think nothing of it if a person screams
his head off, as some sports fans do, at an exciting
football game. But they insist that to be enthusiastic
about Christ and Christianity is evidence of un-
healthy fanaticism.

Such individuals are perfectly willing to think
of Christianity in terms of living a good life, helping others, giving to the Red Cross, and even attending church occasionally. But if you talk to them
about personal devotion to Jesus Christ, or yielded-
ness to the Holy Spirit, or the Second Coming of
our Lord, or future judgment, they are likely to get
restless, examine their watches, and suddenly remember an appointment somewhere else.

Agrippa

King Agrippa was another man who presumed to sit in judgment on Paul. This man has been called "the secular head of the Jewish religion." He had the right to decide who was to be the high priest, and the vestments worn by the high priest on the Day of Atonement were kept in Agrippa's custody. For all his ecclesiastical authority and his knowledge of the Law, Agrippa was a cruel and evil man. Bernice, the mistress with whom he lived, was his own sister. Like Felix, Agrippa didn't allow religion to interfere with his personal pleasures, and his extensive knowledge of the Law had little effect on his morality.

When Festus declared Paul out of his mind, the apostle turned to Agrippa.

"The king knows about these matters," he said, "and I speak to him also with confidence. . . . King Agrippa, do you believe the Prophets? I know that you do!" (vv. 26, 27)

The question really put Agrippa on the spot. If he admitted that he believed the Old Testament prophecies, he would have no excuse for not receiving Jesus as the Messiah, for Jesus' birth, life, and death fulfilled what the prophets had written. On the other hand, if he denied belief in the prophetic writings, he would alienate the Jews with whom he professed to be in sympathy.

The king was not minded to be caught on either horn of this dilemma. He did not answer Paul's question at all, but brushed the matter off with a laugh. "You are trying to make a Christian of me in a few minutes!" he said (cf. v. 28).

"Not you only, but all those who are here today," said Paul, holding up his chained hands. "Oh, if only they were all believers, like me—except for these chains!"

The interview was getting too warm for King Agrippa, and he stood (v. 30) to indicate that it was over. (Have you had the person to whom you witnessed change the subject or leave suddenly?)

A good many people resemble King Agrippa. When confronted with the Gospel they step aside; they refuse to face up to the truth. When you tell them they must come to God for forgiveness through faith in Christ, they say that this is what they now do, or once did, or have always done. Or they brush off the Gospel invitation with some kind of wise-crack—"Are you trying to *convert me?*"—the impli-cation being that conversion is the last thing *they* need. Like Agrippa, they simply refuse to face squarely the most important issue in life.

The Jewish leaders, Felix, Festus, and Agrippa all undertook to pass judgment on Paul, but not one of them was qualified to do so.

• The Jewish leaders wanted the comfortable and profitable *status quo* maintained at all costs. Their way of dealing with unpleasant truth was to kill the person who proclaimed it.

• Felix didn't let his intellectual understand-ing of the Gospel interfere with the sins in which he found so much pleasure. He was a procrasti-nator, too. He put off until "a more convenient sea-son" the disturbing claims of Christ.

• Festus was a fair man and protected Paul from his enemies, but he hadn't an ounce of spiritual discernment. He thought Paul was insane because Christ mattered more to him than anything else in life.

• Agrippa refused to confront truth, too, and hid behind a wisecrack to avoid embarrassment.

These were the men who had the power of life or death over the Apostle Paul, but nothing they said or did could affect the message Paul represented. Truth is truth, no matter what men say or do. And when any man confronts the truth, it is he—not truth—who is on trial.

The sort of persons we've been thinking of are all around us. It may even be that we are tempted, at times, to do less than face squarely the claim of our Lord to all we have and are.

We must avoid such an attitude at all costs!

After Paul had been taken away, Festus and Agrippa held a brief consultation. One thing was clear to them: Paul had done nothing worthy of death or imprisonment (v. 31). However, since he had appealed to Caesar, they felt they must detain him, innocent as he was, and send him on to Rome. How they justified holding a man for an appeal when they had found him innocent we do not know. The technicalities of law are strange and wonderful!

But Paul's great desire to preach in Rome was about to be fulfilled at last. The Roman government delivered him from his enemies and paid his way to the capital.

Some think that when Agrippa went to Rome, not long after he had heard Paul, he spoke to Nero about the apostle and was influential in getting him out of prison (two years later!)

Let's hope so!

25
Shipwrecked
Acts 27

The account of Paul's voyage to Rome is as exciting a narrative as is to be found anywhere in the Bible. It has been called "one of the most instructive documents for the knowledge of ancient seamanship." Even if we merely take it at face value, it is a profitable portion of Scripture.

"Above all," writes Bruce, "it is valuable to us for its portrayal of the character of Paul in circumstances in which the real man is most likely to be revealed. We have seen him in many roles, but here we see him as the practical man in an emergency."

God's servants have often been able, in such times, to give the help or advice that less spiritual men were unable to provide.

Festus had treated Paul much better than Felix, who had let him simmer in jail for two years. A short time, probably, after Agrippa had interviewed the apostle, Festus turned him over to a centurion named Julius to be delivered to Rome.

In the party with Paul were Aristarchus (v. 2; cf. 19:29; 20:4) and Luke (cf. "we," v. 1). Probably these men were not prisoners, but had shipped as friends of the apostle. After his long confinement, Paul must have found the sea voyage, for all its hardships, something of a relief.

The usual sea route from Caesarea to Rome was via Alexandria, Egypt, but in those days one waited for a ship to come along bound in the direction one wanted to go. There were no sailing schedules. The first available vessel was a coastline boat headed for Asia Minor, and on this the party set out, along with an unspecified number of other prisoners, and soldiers to guard them. In all, there were 276 persons, including crew, on board.

At Sidon, Julius gave Paul "shore leave" to visit his friends in the town (cf. v. 3). It is rather remarkable that something is said to the credit of every Roman centurion mentioned in the New Testament.

The voyage was a slow one, for the winds were contrary (v. 4) and the ship had to "tack" against the prevailing west and northwestern breezes. Finally, though, it reached Myra, on the south shore of Asia Minor, then called Asia. There the centurion transferred his prisoners to another vessel, sailing from Egypt to Rome. Egypt was the granary of the Roman Empire, and a sort of imperial merchant marine carried wheat and other grain from Alexandria to Italy.

After a futile wait for favorable winds, the crew took the ship, with some difficulty, as far as Fair Havens, a port on the south side of the island of Crete.

Travel on the eastern part of the Mediterranean shut down about November 11 each fall and was considered hazardous after September 11 for the light craft then in use. The Day of Atonement (cf. v. 9) was already past, so the date must have been mid-October. Favorable weather was not likely to be coming, and as the vessel lay at anchor at Fair Havens, all hands became restless. The captain, or owner, saw his profits for the voyage melting away as he paid the idle crew. The sailors hankered for a port with more "attractions." The soldiers itched to get back to Rome and perhaps their families. Only Paul and his friends, probably, accepted the delay as of the Lord. Ability to accept frustrating delay is a sign of spiritual maturity.

Gloomy Forecast

"Men," Paul told those in charge of the ship, "I perceive that the voyage will certainly be attended with damage and great loss" (v. 10).

It was rather remarkable that the apostle was "in" on the discussion of whether to continue or delay the voyage. Even as a prisoner, he had the respect of his fellow men. The fact that he lived close to the Lord did not keep him from establishing personal relationships with people, and his whole-hearted concern for what is eternal did not make his opinions on "practical" matters less valuable.

The centurion apparently was in command of the ship (v. 11) and made the decisions. Naturally, he was more inclined to accept advice from "expert" navigators than from an itinerant missionary. So "the majority reached a decision to put out to sea from there, if somehow they could reach Phoenix . . . and spend the winter there" (v. 12). Phoenix, on the other side of Crete, had a better harbor than Fair Havens.

This was not the last time a proper course of action was *not* discovered by a majority vote. Such a vote determines what people *think,* but not necessarily what is *right.*

The ship had not been out of the harbor long (v. 14) when a violent wind, with the force of a hurricane, caught it and drove it toward the open sea (v. 15). It was all the crew could do to get the dinghy, a small boat normally towed behind the ship, on board (v. 16).

The next move was to "frap" the ship. The men passed cables under the hull and tightened them to keep the planks from separating and springing leaks. They were afraid they would be driven ashore on the quicksands along the north African coast, the scene of numerous shipwrecks. It does not appear that they were actually in immediate danger from this source, but we can hardly blame them for being mistaken. For more than two weeks they could see neither landmarks, stars, sun, or moon.

The mariners let down a sea anchor, jettisoned some of their wheat cargo (v. 18), and threw the rigging overboard (v. 19). They gradually abandoned all hope of survival (v. 20). Even Paul must have been tempted to be fearful, or the angel would not have told him not to be afraid (v. 24).

The ship on which John Wesley crossed the Atlantic in 1735 ran into a fierce storm. Wesley notes in his diary that he felt "unwilling to die." This troubled him, especially because 26 Moravians on board remained calm and did not seem to worry.

"Weren't you afraid?" Wesley asked one of the Moravian men after the storm had passed.

"I thank God, no," was the reply.

"And your women and children?" asked Wesley.

"Our women and children are not afraid to die, either," replied the Moravian.

This testimony gave Wesley something to pray about, and in due time he conquered his fear.

Perhaps those on board ship with the Apostle Paul marveled at his confidence and courage, due to his belief in the Lord's promise that he would preach in Rome. These qualities may have enabled him to witness effectively to many of his shipmates and to lead some of them to Christ.

In the midst of the crisis, Paul made an announcement. We can appreciate his opening remark, which was the equivalent of "I told you so!" (cf. v. 21). He said this not to gloat but to remind his hearers that he had been right the last ime he had spoken so that they would listen to him this time. And this time he had good news. Though the ship would founder, all hands would be saved (v. 22).

Paul went on to tell how an angel of God had appeared to him during the night, assuring him not only of his own safety, but of the safety of all on the vessel. God had given them to him!

We probably underestimate the blessings that come to all kinds of people through the work of God's servants. Hospitals, schools, and social agencies, though they are the outgrowth of Christianity, minister to the redeemed and to the unregenerate alike. Many a godless man has been spared judgment and brought to repentance and salvation through the prayers of a godly Christian wife. Many a wayward son or daughter had been brought to the foot of the Cross because of the constant intercession of consecrated parents.

Paul could say, "I believe God, that it will turn out exactly as I have been told" (v. 25). He knew the Lord would keep His promises.

Breakers Ahead

The ship had now been blown back and forth for two weeks on the Sea of Adrea (not "the Adriatic"), as the central part of the Mediterranean was then called. At midnight the sailors surmised, perhaps because they heard breakers, that they were approaching land. A couple of soundings confirmed this suspicion. Lest the ship be broken in pieces on the shore, the crew let out four anchors. They longed for daybreak.

Some of the sailors, on the pretext of fastening more anchors to the ship's bow, launched the dinghy with a view to abandoning the ship. They intended to save themselves at the expense of all on the craft.

But Paul saw through their deception. He knew that every able-bodied seaman would be needed in the morning to handle the ship, so he warned the centurion to interrupt the sailors' plans to leave.

At the beginning of the voyage, Paul was a prisoner in the hands of the centurion. The next day, he was at liberty to visit his friends (v. 3). Next he was giving advice (and *good* advice, too) about the voyage (v. 10). Later, he encouraged the crew by reporting his vision (vv. 21-25). Then he advised the centurion about the escaping crewmen. By this time he was practically in command of the vessel! He is a testimony to the world's need for wisdom that is from above.

As day dawned, Paul reminded his shipmates that they had eaten nothing for the past two weeks. Getting ashore would be a strenuous business, and they would desperately need all the strength they could muster. He urged them to eat (v. 34), and he set an example, breaking bread and eating it.

In full view of the passengers and crew, Paul asked God's blessing over his breakfast. Do *you* ask God to bless the food when you eat in public, or would doing so embarrass you?

After they had strengthened themselves with the food, all hands set about lightening the ship, throwing the rest of the wheat overboard to give the vessel every chance of riding high in the sea and so reaching shore safely. There are crisis times when we become quite willing to sacrifice what was once vastly important to us. Stress has a way of changing our system of values.

The crew did not recognize the land they saw when day broke, but they decided to beach the ship in a small sandy bay. When they had cast off their anchors, however, the high waves stranded the ship on a sand bar. The vessel broke in two and the stern sank.

The soldiers, who would answer with their lives for the prisoners, wanted to put them all to death to prevent any escapes. This was standard operating practice. The centurion, however, probably out of fondness for Paul, refused to allow such inhuman treatment. He ordered all prisoners who could swim to get to land at once, and told the rest to make their way to the beach on anything they could find that would float them. And so "they all were brought safely to land" (v. 44), just as God had promised.

Had it not been for Paul, 276 lives would have been lost with this grain ship that sailed too late in the season. Paul's practical advice was responsible for saving these lives. His advice was accepted because those who traveled with him had come to know him, to respect him, and to trust him—and probably to *like* him. They knew he was sincere in his concern for them. They knew he had access to a source of strength and wisdom about which they knew nothing.

Our age in general, and young people in particular, demand a Christianity that is *practical*. It is important that we recognize that the historic Christian faith is highly relevant to the very real problems of daily life *today*. It speaks to the needs of farmers, bankers, industrialists, and storekeepers, as well as educators, housewives, students, and retirees. Paul, on his voyage to Rome, is an example of how a believer should face *any* kind of crisis.

Sometimes Christians gain influence in other fields than the Church by sacrificing a strong Christian stand, but this was not Paul's policy. He was willing to be all things to all men. He had no problems about making insignificant concessions in order to win others to Christ. But he never compromised his convictions.

Paul, this chapter makes clear, was appreciated for what he *was* rather than for what he *believed*. Sometimes Christians seem to think they should be esteemed by others simply because they hold the Christian faith, but this is not true. The respect of others must be *earned*.

Paul shows how.

26
Rome at Last!
Acts 28

Paul and his companions, after making their way ashore from their sinking ship, learned that they were on the island of Malta (the word means "refuge"), about 100 miles south of Sicily, below the Italian boot.

The natives on the island, though "barbarous" (v. 2, AV) in the sense that they did not speak Greek, were warmhearted and friendly. The travelers had been drenched in the waves and a cold rain was falling, but these practical-minded natives kindled a fire and did what they could to make their uninvited guests comfortable.

The newssheet of a Christian organization, after the disastrous floods that swept parts of the eastern United States in the wake of Hurricane Agnes in 1972, urged employees to "Pray for flood victims." This is good wholesome advice, of course, but often prayer should be accompanied by material help.

What do *you* do when you read about some great disaster? Do you pray briefly for those involved, shake your head sadly, and wish you could do more? You *can!* Money provides a way of helping disaster victims even at the far ends of the earth, and there are organizations ready to use it under Christian auspices, giving the Gospel along with the "practical" help. And don't think that because you can't give largely you are justified in not giving at all!

Paul himself realized the importance of active help. He set about collecting a fagot of sticks to keep the fire going. No job was too menial for the apostle, and he was willing to be useful in material as well as spiritual ways.

Among the sticks that Paul collected was a viper that had been dormant from the cold weather. It was revived by heat from the fire, and struck suddenly, fastening itself on the apostle's hand. There are no poisonous snakes on Malta today, but it is not likely the natives were mistaken about the wild life of their own island. In any case, as one commentator says, the interesting part of the story is not the poisonous nature of the snake but the poisonous nature of the conclusions the natives drew about it. They whispered to one another, "This man is obviously a murderer! He has escaped from the sea, but justice will not let him live" (v. 4, PH).

Paul nonchalantly shook the viper into the fire (cf. Mark 16:18) while the natives looked for him to swell up or suddenly fall down dead (Acts 28:6).

Do we ever put someone down as a secret sinner because he meets with an automobile accident, financial reverses, or domestic difficulties? It is true that sometimes sickness or other misfortune comes as a result of sin, but often it has no more connection with guilt than the viper had with Paul's morals. Judgment is God's business, and we had better let *Him* attend to it!

Change of Mind

After the natives waited a long time and nothing happened to Paul, they changed their minds and concluded that he was a God. Our evaluation of a person may go up and down like an elevator if we judge him by superficial evidence.

The "first man" of the island, Publius by name, charitably opened his home to Paul and his friends and entertained them for three days. Hospitality to strangers is an art that Christians especially are to cultivate (Heb. 13:2). One can begin to practice it by inviting into one's home visitors or new members from one's church.

We *may* "entertain angels unawares"! Publius did! Paul, his guest, prayed for Publius' sick father, and the man was healed (v. 8).

This miracle practically set Paul up as a doctor, and every sick person on the island came to him and found healing. There is no advertisement more effective than a man who has regained his health. Even the spiritual healing of a person who has undergone the miracle of salvation is often less spectacular than a physical healing, because the change is less conspicuous.

It was said of Peter Parker, of the American Board of Missions, who founded a Christian hospital in Canton, China, about 1830, that "he opened China at the point of a lancet." Paul did not even need a lancet. His healings were the direct work of God.

The shipwreck victims stayed on Malta three months, until spring. When the left, the thoughtful and grateful natives again showed their practical concern by supplying them all the necessities they had lost when their ship went down (v. 10). They also gave them many "marks of respect," which could be translated "honoraria" (cf. 1 Tim. 5:17, 18).

Julius, the centurion, put his prisoners on another grain ship, which took them and its cargo to Puteoli, one of the two main grain ports for ships from Alexandria. Here Julius allowed Paul to spend a week with "some brethren" (v. 14) in the area.

Then came the last lap of the journey. While the party was still some 30 or 40 miles from Rome, a group of Christians from that city came down the highway to meet Paul and escort him to his destination. "When Paul saw them he thanked God and took courage." He had been in prison for two long years. It heartened him to know that in Rome there were those who shared his faith, were not ashamed to be identified with an accused man, and would give him the Christian fellowship he so needed in this crisis.

God's people today are often in desperate need of such encouragement. They need to know that in their personal crises there are fellow Christians standing with them. It isn't enough that we pray for one another. We need to *let a troubled brother know* how much we care. These Roman Christians walked 60 or 80 miles so that the apostle would be aware of their love. Are we willing to do the inconvenient thing—to go out of our way as the Roman believers did—to communicate our concern?

Paul had dreamed for at least three years of getting to Rome. His great, unselfish ambition was to take the Gospel of Christ to the Eternal City, the crossroads of the Empire, the capital of the political world of his day. And now, under circumstances perhaps not quite what he would have chosen, he was there! From Jerusalem to Rome had been a long journey and a hard one, but God had seen him through.

Paul was allowed to live in a house at his own expense. He was chained to an imperial guardsman (v. 16) but was free to have visitors.

Paul and the Jews

Paul had regularly preached "to the Jew first," and he continued this policy in Rome. He rested for three days and then invited the leading Jews of the city to his lodgings. He told them that his arrest and imprisonment were the work of the Jerusalem Jews but that he had done nothing against them or their customs. They had turned him over to the Romans, who examined him and would have released him as innocent (v. 18) had not the Jews objected. This had forced him to appeal to Caesar, but he had *not* appealed because of any complaint against his own people.

Paul emphasized that there was no anti-Semitism in his heart. He harbored no grudge against the Jews. (Do *you?*)

"I am wearing this chain," he concluded, "for the sake of the hope of Israel" (v. 20). Many of the non-Christian Jews still cherished the Messianic hope but did not believe Jesus had fulfilled the prophecies of their Scriptures.

The Jews said they had no communication from Palestine, either written or in person, making charges against Paul (v. 21). They said they would like to meet with him and hear his views. They had heard about Christianity, of course, and it was spoken against everywhere.

On the appointed day they came back to his

quarters in large numbers, and from morning until evening he talked to them. On the basis of their own Law and Prophets, he explained the Messianic claims of Jesus Christ.

"Some were convinced; others refused to believe" (v. 24, WEY). We may be certain, in view of what follows, that this refusal to believe was deliberate. Faith is not simply an unbidden emotion. It can be the product of the will. You *can* make up your mind to believe—if you *want* to. These Jews *would* not believe (v. 24).

A missionary to the Jews reports that it is harder to work with a group of Hebrews than with an individual. They will make a decision together if all are fully persuaded, but as they discuss a matter among themselves, the objection of one is likely to influence the others. This was Paul's experience, but as his guests were getting ready to leave he had the last word, and it was a devastating one. He quoted Isaiah 6:9, 10. "You will keep on hearing, but will not understand; and you will keep on seeing, but will not perceive; for the heart of this people has become dull, and with their ears they scarcely hear, and they have closed their eyes; lest they should see with their eyes and hear with their ears, and understand with their heart and turn again, and I should heal them" (Acts 28:26, 27).

The implication of this passage is that hardness and dullness of heart are results of deliberate rejection of truth. Those who *will* not believe come to the point where they are no longer *able* to believe. They hear the message but they cannot understand it. They see the truth but cannot perceive it. It has become meaningless to them.

"If any man have ears to hear, let him hear [understand]", urged the Lord Jesus (Mark 4:23). We are to exercise our God-given faculties for spiritual understanding. To refuse to do so, or to procrastinate and wait until some future time, is dangerous. "Now is the acceptable time; behold, *now* is the day of salvation" (2 Cor. 6:2). To postpone making a decision can be as fatal as to reject Christ.

A few scholars take the Isaiah passage to mean that God arbitrarily makes it impossible for some persons to believe, but it is clear from Paul's use of the Scripture that the hardening and dullness in view are brought on by deliberate rejection of truth.

The "therefore" of verse 28 looks back to verses 26 and 27. Since the Jews were turning away from the Gospel by their persistent rejection, God's salvation would be proclaimed to the Gentiles, many of whom would receive it.

When we fail to take advantage of opportunities God gives us to serve Him, He will find others to do His work and win His approval. If some do not believe and make His Son their Saviour, others will. The wedding feast will be well supplied with guests (Matt. 22). The Jews did not come, but the Gentiles did. If you don't, another will!

Paul, chained to his guard, lived in Rome for two years awaiting trial. His heart was full of courage and praise. He wrote, "I want you to know, brethren, that my circumstances have turned out for the greater progress of the Gospel . . . and that most of the brethren, trusting in the Lord because of my imprisonment, have far more courage to speak the Word of God without fear" (Phil. 1:12-14).

Paul witnessed to his guards, and many of them became Christians. He witnessed to his visitors. No doubt many discouraged Christians called on Him and were strengthened by his hearty advice.

224 / The Acts—Then and Now

This is where the inspired record of The Acts comes to an end, but we know from the rest of the New Testament and from other sources (such as the writings of the Church Fathers), that Paul used some of his time to write letters. We call four of them Philemon, Colossians, Ephesians, and Philippians.

We know, too, that because the Palestinian Jews never got to Rome with their complaints against Paul, the apostle was released. The Roman government took a dim view of frivolous prosecutions, and the Jews probably thought it safer simply to let their "case" against Paul die. So Paul was set free.

For more than four years he traveled through Asia Minor, revisiting his beloved converts. It is quite likely that he went also to Spain, on the fringes of the then-known world. He may have gone to Jerusalem again, too. And he wrote 1 Timothy and Titus during those years.

Then he was rearrested and returned to Rome. This time he was treated "as a malefactor" and given no privileges. For long months he languished in a damp dungeon, writing 2 Timothy to his beloved "son" in the Lord.

Finally this selfless man of God was tried, condemned, and beheaded. His body was buried in the catacombs, but his spirit went to glory and received a crown of righteousness (2 Tim. 4:8).

The work the Holy Spirit carried on through Paul, however, did not cease. Down through the centuries to our own day, God continues, through His people, the task of taking the good news of salvation to all men everywhere.